CU2939 Develop Health and Safety and Risk Manage Policies, Procedures and Practices in Health and Social Care or Children and Young People's Settings

1 Understand the current legislativeframework and organisationalhealth, safety and riskmanagement policies, proceduresand practices that are relevant tohealth, and social care or childrenand young people's settings.

Health and safety is an act which envelops all aspects of our day to day lives in whatever environment we are in. Focusing on work everybody must comply with the health and safety at work regulations but employers with 5 or more staff must complete risk assessments. Health and safety is a duty of care, looking after the clients, staff, visitors, home, equipment and environment. This will also be taken off site while out in the community. Health and safety is a legal requirement and failure to comply with the law could result in fines, jail or closure for those mistreating act and injury, harm, poor conditions or even death for those on the receiving end of poor health and safety.

So who's responsible? Every resident has a responsibility to keep themselves and others safe and notify staff of any potential hazards. Staff have responsibility for anyone within the home, protecting them from any hazards that could arise in the setting, also using the equipment's and ppe provided to protect themselves. Staff also have the responsibility of attending courses provided, recording injuries, faults and only using equipment when trained to do so. Following the risk assessments in place. The manager has further responsibilities to those listed above, making sure staff are trained and supervised, the work place is suitable and safe to work in, and all equipment is provided and fit for purpose. The manager will also liaise with official bodies at regular times for testing and inspection purposes. Head office and maintenance department have a responsibility to maintain the home carrying out repairs and replacing broken items when required. They will oversee all aspects of the home compliance within the health and safety at work regulations along with the manager of the home.

We follow many regulations in the home which form the health and safety act. These are health and safety at work regulations, personal protective equipment regulation; this covers all equipment for personal protection (gloves, aprons, masks, goggles, boots, shoe protectors, visors, hats or helmets) making sure they are available, fit for use and used correctly through training. Provision and use of work equipment regulations (puwer) this regulation is about equipment used and the testing of equipment making sure it's tested by a trained individual and is fit for use. Manual handling operations regulations govern all aspects of manual handling from staff training to equipment used, insuring staff are trained on manual handling and how to use the equipment, but again making sure the equipment is used for correct purposes and maintained. There are many regulations, Riddor, Coshh, first aid, food safety act and medicines regulation. All the regulations must be met by law according to stipulations in the regulations. We carry out supervisions, training, risk assessment, spot checks, reviews and audits to maintain compliance of all regulations.

1.2
How does my service meet the requirements set out in legislation regarding health and safety? One of the ways we look at this is to follow the essential standards set out by the care quality commission relating to health and safety.

Regulation 9 outcome 4 care and welfare of people who use services, in my service we complete this outcome by having our person centered approach, all care plans follow a basic format but the information in them are unique and personal to the individual having weekly schedules and activities just for them. We ensure that maintenance is carried out when required in the home. Lighting, heating and décor in individual's rooms are personalised by thermostat on radiator and personal belongings from rugs to curtains adorn the rooms. The home prefers to keep neutral colour scheme in rooms for painting but the client picks furnishings to add colour. Medications will be administered at set times throughout the day in clients preferred situation, in room or meds area. Main meals are prepared and made available at certain times throughout the day, at other times residents can make their own foods with assistance from staff if required.

Regulation 10 outcome 16, assessing and monitoring the quality of service provision, this get carried out in several ways with residents and family we have regular meetings and are always available to talk to if anyone wants to discuss anything. We send out quality surveys every year which allows for a reflective practice. Other services come and visit are clients or ourselves and discuss how things are and weather anything can be done further to assist clients. We are awaiting dignity in care to come and visit to show we have a person centred approach and provide a dignified service. We have inspections yearly by council monitoring contracts, they inspect every aspect of service from client's wellbeing to meds protocols and everything else in between. Staff have regular supervisions and undergo yearly appraisals as well as monthly meetings which all allow for feedback and input to be communicated. Audits and maintenance are carried out, most audits are every month and reflect on occurrences from previous month with outcomes that will have to be improved within a timescale set out. Maintenance will visit weekly and carry out as many maintenance issues we have then every year will carry out pat testing, legionella and fire testing.

Regulation 11 outcome 7 safeguarding people who use services from abuse, staff are all trained every year on safeguarding and have all read the safeguard policy. The whistleblowing policy is also read and the procedure is displayed in every unit. Staff are trained in safeguarding as a whole, some staff have also completed like me an alerter course, referrer course and trainer course which allows me to train others in safeguarding. We also complete 60 sec training which is a brief session to keep staffs minds on their responsibility. Incident reports and ABC charts are completed with any instance of abuse and cqc notifications if required, all of which we have completed supervision on.

2 Be able to implement and monitor compliance with health, safety and risk management requirements in health and social care or children and young people's settings.

2.1 & 2.2

Prior to employment commencement at my service staff will undertake a DBS check have references checked and an interview. During the interview the candidate will have a tour of the home and facilities available. If successful in interview and employment is offered new staff will receive an employee handbook which will state clearly their roles and responsibilities within health and safety within the workplace. On the first day of work the new employee will be again shown around the home giving greater gratis on the health and safety looking at fire points and evacuation being shown the power room and gas cut off. The new employee will shadow staff for the first couple of weeks getting to understand and know the clients, paperwork, recording, and the job. Within the first twelve weeks of employment staff will undertake the core induction standards training, this has many aspects of training with an emphasis in two units on health and safety, this will cover coshh, fire safety, moving and handling, ppe, first aid, riddor and food safety there will be sections on safeguarding and whistleblowing. We will continue training throughout employment on these topics and more with regular refreshers to keep knowledge refreshed and accurate. Every year when the policies and procedures get updated from head office staff are asked to read and sign with any new key information being addressed within the staff meeting. Care plans are wrote for clients on initially coming into the service and updated with new information as more is known and communicated by clients. Risk assessments on clients will be wrote with previous knowledge or knew information when in service and updated regular with minimum update to both risk assessments and care plans every year which will be carried out by senior staff members. Audits are carried out monthly looking at areas such as care plans, medication, room checks, safeguarding's, falls and complaints. Building risk assessment are carried out every 6 months and pat tests, fire checks are done every year from trained maintenance staff. Every week the trained staff will do fire testing and every 6 months fire evacuations occur with new risk assessments undertaken every time. We have a maintenance book in the office that staff will fill out with any issues requiring work. The accident books are kept in office and staff fill them out along with incident reports, falls charts and injury sheets dependant on injury sustained. If required medical services will be called and cqc notifications will be completed. Riddor will be contacted if the need arises. As well as staff abiding by health and safety everyone that enters our building has a duty under the health and safety regulations to protect themselves and others from harm, report any issues within the home and not to cause harm or potential hazards. Fire alarms are tested every Wednesday around 11am and any visitors are informed prior of pending alarm. Staff are in each unit and the office so are always available for any visitors should they have any comments or concerns. When entering building visitors will ring doorbell for entry and will be escorted to who they want to see. Residents in the home have a duty to assist in maintaining cleanliness within the home primarily their rooms, the clients are asked daily to empty bins and any potential hazards. Clients know that the fire doors should not be obstructed and nothing is to be left out in hallway or communal area that could possible become fire hazard or trip hazard. Under our cosh policy staff remove cosh and is taken with them to area to be cleaned then put away back into cosh room never left out. Due to our clientele with mental health visitors are asked if they want to be alone with a resident or have staff present. Any workmen are supervised around the building with staff as protection for both parties.

2.3

When health and safety is working well we have no concerns but when practice and procedures are not complied with we have to take action. The list of possible non-compliance of health and safety issues within the home could be endless so I will look at a few examples and describe actions we as a home and organisation would do.

Moving and handling is always an issue that people lose focus on, a client falls over doesn't seem hurt and asks to be helped up. Policy and training will tell us to firstly assess person in situate for any physical harm, if deemed ok then an object like a chair is manoeuvred in place and staff talk the client through stages to stand, guiding resident up with a steady hand on shoulder and back till stable. If unable to stand unaided then a lift aid like a hoist will be used by two trained individuals to assist client up. This is good practice however it has been known for staff to assist with hands and pull individuals to feet with assistance or give an arm for support, this is poor practice. If we see this occurrence within the home we would stop it immediately and assist in proper manner. The staff members training will be looked at if completed moving and handling training and is current in this then they will be asked why they have done so. The likely outcome will be further training and supervision and possible note to file (stage 1 disciplinary). If a moving and handling error occurs again within 12 months then the staff member will be under investigation and could face dismissal for poor practice.

Coshh products being left unattended is a serious breach of health and safety within our home. Currently because of an incident that occurred we changed the home policy that all coshh must be with staff at all times while using it then returned to locked cupboard when used. All staff within the home are aware of policy and safeguarding currently in place, it's documented in several staff meetings and has been discussed regular with all staff. If coshh was found unattended at any point within the home in an area that any one could obtain it then the staff involved would immediately be investigated and either final warning or dismissal will be looked at as this is gross misconduct.

Other less severe issues arise but could have great consequence for example someone wearing gloves for cleaning then conduct personal care wearing same gloves. This again is looked at in trainings such as coshh and infection control and is a fundamental aspect of care. Consequences of cross contamination or harm to others can occur and yes sometimes people get busy and are called in to help then don't think but the potential for harm is great. This circumstance would warrant a discussion of what occurred and why it shouldn't and possible supervisions to alert not to do again.

Any health and safety concern in the home that is not complied with could have negative effects on the home the hse could put into place guidance, improvement notice or prohibition in more severe cases closure or being sent to jail for non-compliance. It is everybody's responsibility for health and safety and even when you think you are helping or there's an emergency we need to stop assess breathe adapt and then do job.

2.4

Records in respect of health and safety are one of the most important things. All records must be dated, timed, factual, clear, and signed. We must follow the usual data protection procedures of not using names if appropriate and only share with those that require information to carry out job. Any accident should be in accident book, incident report in folder and faxed to care team, family informed, if required cqc notification, safeguarding and riddor could be involved. If incident occurred then incident reports must be filled if the police have been involved then again teams and family will be notified and cqc notification. Fire assessments must be recorded weekly and 6 monthly evacuations and yearly code testing by maintenance all these should be recorded when complete with any issues arising recorded, reported and fixed by appropriate person.

Mar charts are kept for 5 years and all returns are lodged for same time period. We audit monthly on many aspects this helps to keep records up to date and together. Inspectors when visiting will be able to see the audits as a good tool to quickly identify concerns and to see whether it has been addressed. All records undertaken by anyone in this employ could be taken to court under any investigation and can be used as part testimony so must be factual and completed by those who actually witnessed/ or did the thing recorded. Having clear precise systems in place streamline the effectiveness and allows all staff to have the knowledge of what is required.

3 Be able to lead the implementation of policies, procedures and practices to manage risk to individuals and others in health and social care or children and Young people's settings.

To develop new policies, procedures or practice for the home or residents requires looking at the situations that have arisen that require this change to occur.
Usually there is need for something to be put into place to manage situations that have a hazard or risk. The process we would look at is a risk assessment. This tool can be used as a generic thing that's protects and helps everyone or could be needed for a certain task or be involved for certain individuals. Even a generic risk assessment can be tweaked to be compliant for individual basis just like the pregnancy risk assessment, this is basic and generic and is adapted for the individual through consultation.

Risk assessments should contain the relevant information this consists of what is the hazard (anything that could cause harm), who potentially this could affect (the home, a group of people or an individual person) and how it could affect them (medical problems, physical harm or mental harm). We then have to ascertain the risk (the probability of the hazard occurring and causing harm). The next step would be to look at precautions (things that could help minimise or even eliminate the risk occurring). With most risk assessments we record outcomes and implement them into practice, this allows the review procedure to occur at the interval deemed necessary, this means it must be carried out in that time but could be done earlier and more often. Some risk assessments we don't write down but we undertake several times a day these are called dynamic risk assessments and we use them in our day to day lives on everything we do like crossing a road, we get to the road assess the conditions and evaluate the risk of the hazard happening then cross when safe to do so, this is the risk assessment procedure. Some people we care for however can't do this themselves and potentially could be hurt so we would do a risk assessment, supervision and the aim is to get the individual able to do so themselves.

If the risk is great and becomes something that affects the whole service then our company might introduce a policy or procedure to follow based on your risk assessment recommendations.

3.2 &3.3

How do we manage potential risks and hazards? In my setting our care plans are set into 13 sections the first three are based on daily reports, information and contacts the next ten break down the clients care into sections for example physical health, mobility, eating and drinking and mental health. Using the information gathered prior to admission and information gained from service user and family we complete the care plan front sheets (see appendix) which on completion it allows for us to identify personal risks and the severity of the risk. We have generic risk assessment for ever client; example being risk of harm with toiletries, this would be in the hygiene section. For every section in the care plan we have risk assessments that we could use as basic template and adapt with the information gathered to each individual requiring them. Not everyone in care are going to require risk assessments personally to manage their care.

Having a person centred approach while writing care plans allow for a more detailed care plan and risk acknowledgement and manageability of the risks. We always have to keep in mind what potentially we see as harmless could really put someone in harm's way so identifying these risks as regular systems to care plan writing is very important to all involved.

4 Be able to promote a culture where needs and risks are balanced with health and safety practice in health and social care or children and young people's settings.

4.1 &4.2

Should people in care settings be able to undertake an activity because it's risky or dangerous? Let's change that question and ask why they shouldn't?
As care providers we like the term risk enablement not risk management, our job of supporting individuals is to help clients live a fulfilled life not one that is surrounded by red tape saying stop. Doing what is wanted through choice has to balance with best interest and health and safety this usually means limiting risks and giving informed choice.
Positive risk taking is that not what we all do in our life's we know that things could hurt us but we want to do it anyway, so we enquire, we learn and when we have weighed up the outcomes and still want to do things, we do it having the knowledge of what could happen good and bad. Some people will say that our job is protection and we should never put someone in harm's way why? Human rights human passion human interests make us want to do things. Stopping someone from doing something because the possibility of getting hurt could isolate the individual and could inevitably make someone go and do the activity without the information, help and support.
Everyone should have the right to do what makes them happy, taking time to sit evaluate and inform. Weigh up the options and possibly find safer ways of achieving goals takes a little time and a little effort but brings in great rewards for the individuals we look after.

Looking at being person centred again while creating positive risk choices allows the client to gain the best possible care from any situation. We must have an ethos a good staff group, enablers to assist and perform with the clients or the client possibly will go without and this becomes poor practice. There will be times that the staff, family and others might find the situation is too risky, this needs balance will the benefit outweigh the cost sometimes the answer is no but there may be closer alternatives that could be better it just takes the staff to enquire and research to do the best with and for the clients we support.

4.3 & 4.4

When looking at our staff we employ a diverse range of employees with different interest and beliefs. This promotes a diverse service and a more unique service. Every client we look after is different have different values and interests and require a personalised service. Balancing opportunity with risks means being proportionate and realistic. Knowing limits to people's abilities can be hard especially with our group of clients. Some clients have asked to attend activities which I personally would never want to do, this is my fear but I can't transfer this to that individual. Having the rights to do what they want to is a key principle of ours. My responsibility here would be to enable the individual this entails researching the activity, this includes locations, prices, risks and any other information about topic. Having the information lets the client and I know realistically what is entailed. Once all the data is collected we can discuss with the service user the possible risks and opportunities involved in the activity. My beliefs and fears shouldn't come into the equation but I would make it clear that I wouldn't attend but will find someone who will. Once we have discussed the data we plan, we do a risk assessment outlining the possible risks and ways to manage the risks involved. Part of the risk assessment would include finances as clients will fund these themselves and some will require a budgeting plan, this itself becomes a risk due to weather they will financially commit to the activity, we have to be realistic in timescale to save the monies and that makes us realistic in timescale to attend activity. The risk assessment may be altered several times between originally being written and attending activity because needs change and we will regularly review this with service user. My service has a can do attitude towards choices and risks but we are realistic and proportional with the clients abilities we will always endeavour to complete and wishes and support their choice and independence even if family belief its unwise, our job is to support the individual, give them the opportunity, the information and guidance and facilitate any opportunity they choose to do.

Assisting the clients to fulfil hopes and dreams promotes self worth, gives a sense of purpose and fulfilment. Allowing for the client to manage and understand the hazards and risks involved again make them feel important enabled and worthy even if choosing not to attend they become happy knowing it was their choice. The clients get a better awareness of what activities entail the risks, the cost and realistic timescales to attend activities. This person centred approach improves happiness and a more rounded service promoting clients choice and independence, this allows for funding providers to establish that are service is good and unique and may entail further referrals to our service.

5 Be able to improve health, safety and risk management policies, procedures and practices in health and social care or children and young people's settings.

We may very well belief we are providing a quality service and meeting requirements to the regulations in the health and safety act but monitoring these and obtaining feedback is the only ways to actually know we are, we obtain feedback and monitor regular using tools and feedback from agencies to keep standards and improve if require. CQC and local social service complete regular inspections where they look at every aspect of the care we provide. They will look at staff files and residents care plans, talk to staff and residents, look at all records like HACCP and meds records also overlooking our audits and other records which will include registration, insurance and maintenance records. We as a service by law have to provide openness of our records and service to the investigators providing all documentation and records they require. CQC and social services will give initial feedback on the service especially if they believe improvement or alterations are required. Following the inspection the service will receive a full feedback document from the agency with their outcomes, we luckily have only ever been asked for minor changes to our service which included putting into place a monitoring system for HACCP books.

Other agencies also inspect our service these include dignity in care, the fire brigade and food standards agency, the chemist may also inspect to see weather are medication process is up to date and in good standard. All the agencies inspect different areas of our service and seek compliance to regulations in health and safety. Dignity in care looks at having a dignified person centred service, making sure things are assessable and meeting needs and choices of those we care for. The fire brigade will look at all aspects of fire within the home from the fire book, evacuation procedure and route, risk assessments for whole home and individuals, the brigade will also inspect the maintenance records, extinguishers and exits. They will establish compliance or anything required to do to comply. Food standards agency visit every year and inspect HACCP and the kitchen within the home they will suggest any improvements required and will score the service on the current standard within the home. The chemist will visit and look at the medicines storage, the returns procedure and overall compliance of meds, the chemist will give feedback and suggest anything that could help with our systems, and legally the chemist only makes suggestions because we invite them they are not a legal body.

Other professionals visit our service like social workers and cpn's they will look at what is required for their service users needs and requirements, this will look at safeguarding aspects as well which comes under health and safety, feedback and suggestions of what might need to be done or done well by the home for the service user will co expressed by these professionals.
The home send out yearly questionnaires to families and care teams which asks how our service is performing through different aspects and allows for any feedback to be recorded. We will check all questionnaire results record them through audits and use any feedback to improve service. The audits carried out every month shows how we are performing in areas within the home and anything that we need to look at to improve. These will include looking at medicines and room checks which look at both cleanliness and maintenance issues in the

home. The comments and complaints are recorded in the complaints book in the office and get audited every month. Complaints, comments and compliments are provided by anyone in the service, visitors or even the public and again allow us to improve systems and promote better practice within the home.

We have meetings every month both resident meetings and staff meetings these will allow for feedback from those using the service and those working in the service to improve standards and systems used. Promoting good working practice giving a personalised service and improving conditions for all involved, this will promote a good working environment stop staff turnover and increase productivity through the staff and make clients happier, promote a good service and increase referrals in service. Supervisions are carried out in different aspects in the training requirements and allow both supervisor and supervisee to acknowledge any potential hazards or risks found during this process.

5.2, 5.3 & 5.4

Evaluating our systems put into place I believe we cover all checks under health and safety but leave room for improvement on monitoring these systems. We currently complete audits every month in falls, safeguarding, room checks, medication, infection control, care planning, complaints. The senior team complete these at the start of every month evaluation the previous month and any outstanding issues from months prior to that. Fire alarms our checked weekly the same as the kitchen hazard analysis critical control points, food hygiene and fridge/freezer/food temps checked daily.
 Medication checks are completed daily. Every two weeks I order coshh and complete checks to establish we have everything required and are suitable for purpose. Part of the coshh is first aid equipment checks and ppe comes under coshh. Maintenance complete regular legionella, pat testing and fire checks which are in the maintenance bible. The staff complete 6 monthly building risk assessment and fire evacuations checking maintenance records at the same time to ascertain records are up to date. Seniors check care plans against room cleans and will complete supervisions to make sure room cleans are completed per rota. Risk assessment and care planning is carried out a minimum of 12 months.
 We have certain actions put in place to monitor aspects are carried out when required, I believe we follow these very well but currently have information in different areas which could get missed if manager or seniors where ill or not trained enough to know requirements of job. The staff group are trained every year on key aspects of health and safety and is recorded on our training charts which highlight any shortfalls in the training requirements, my job is to identify these needs and train staff in these areas. The process is carried out each and every month but I am unable at times to train everyone at the dates required due to shift patterns, holidays and sickness.
 This to me is an area that requires attention and feels that the other senior needs training to a standard that could train the other staff but be reportable to myself to centralise the training. I also believe that each staff meeting should carry an aspect of health and safety even just a few quick fire questions to check knowledge is up to date and legislation is met. This would allow for any changes in policy and procedures to be highlighted and the entire staff group to be informed, and signing the meeting notes states they are aware from a legal standpoint of the changes.

CU2940 Work in Partnership in Health and Social Care or Children and Young People's Settings
1 Understand partnership working.

Partnership working is relatively new with policies only being formed in the 1980's calling for joined up services, the push for the collaboration led to an influx of white papers in the 90's detailing proposals on quality and partnership which ultimately led to the health act in 1999. The health act put duties on health and social services to cooperate and have joint working, this allowed for a combined goal of well being rather than health looking after illness and social looking after dependence. The ultimate goal is person centred care giving the individual more choice a stronger voice and clarity on the care to be delivered.

There are many features of partnership working all were designed with the purpose of streamlining systems of support within health and social care.

Each area where divided into trusts to manage their own finances and delivers the care required.

Health services and social services had to deliver services together because they are linked inevitable one manages the current illness while the other would manage the care after, this done separately causes chaos because there were no sharing and put emphasis on the patient to do all the work which usually wouldn't happen due to lack of information, insight or ability. Sharing the information between services allowed for health to treat the illness and pass care on to social services with little or no delay in the care requirements. This enabled the patient to have the care they needed by the systems they needed in a way which was assessable to them.

Data protection is a fundamental aspect of partnership working the individuals rights to privacy, having a service that is completing as one that is health and social care allowed for the flow of information between the two areas freely following the data laws, rather than records separated in services that may depend on the others information to treat the individual as a whole.

1.2

The big society David Cameron's empowerment for clinicians to improve on collaborating in the services. This was to develop commissioning bodies to be responsible for certain areas of care like dementia services.

In today's society we rely on partnership working in every aspect of the care profession, we often don't realise how much it is used and its uses. Partnership working is so important to deliver the very best care possible for individuals we look after and providing the person centred care which allows the individuals to provide information and promote the care they wish for.

We work with many different professional services as well as our colleagues, partnership working is not perfect and not equal as some professionals will have greater importance than others.

Colleagues and ourselves must work together provide handovers and information flow, use the same care techniques and methods, record, report and use the each other's skills. This will give a dignified person centred care practice that follows our policies and the care plans of each service user, allowing for support from staff, appropriate training and affective partnerships.

Medical services we work with can differ in both importance and requirements for information. GP services will have all medical records for that person and any appointments they have used within the NHS sector, they will also be kept up to date from the mental health teams of the outcomes and requirements, this makes them the key care component and we liaise with them on any medical needs, so our clients and our relationship with GP is the most important. Mental health is my sector so teams within that area will also have great input for example consultants, CPN's, social workers. These groups will need to know the medical requirements that relate to mental health and any social needs but wouldn't need to know all the medical details that occur. The mental health profession is important to our clients as this will keep them mentally healthy and be able to access services they require, so having good partnership working again provides the best possible care being person centred and beneficial for the clients being looked after.

There are many other services used day in and day out whether medical or social and these will only require partial data sharing but all have an importance in the clients well being so have an effective role to play within the partnership care package. Dentist, chiropodist, dietician and physiotherapist all have roles to play in the care given and without them the client wouldn't have all the needs that is required but these services are more minor so have less importance in the partnership hierarchy the information shared to them are purposely only directed at that area of expertise, and these services don't need to know the day to goings on of the clients care.

The other side of health is social and there are many services we use in social some are daycentres, hairdressers, shops and libraries. These services as a whole again have a role within the well being of the clients but generally don't need any information about the client except daycentres who need to know the client, their diagnosis and likes/ dislikes and importance's to client. Daily information flow will occur on activities done, behaviours and general health, this is due to the care being transferred for a period of time to the daycentre. Having good working relationships allow for greater personalisation of the care package, clients needs being known and met.

Overall partnership working is important for clients well being to stop isolation and harm occurring, allows for greater knowledge and independence. The services are able to share information more easily providing better personalised care and easier obtained services for those we look after.

Part of any partnership working is having joint objectives using systems that cross over different services which allows for a standardised care system although are uniquely provided to each individual.

1.3

We obtain better outcomes from partnership working due to providing a person centred care package or personalisation agenda which is where individuals we support define their own requirements. The idea is that the key aspects of fundamental care is that the individual is in the centre of the care choices they work closely with the carers whether that be family or a care home. They are the main relationship and must always remain as so because they coordinate all the care and will know all the ins and outs of the individual and their care needs. This will move further out to further services as doctors and other professionals. To deliver the best service requires the best relationships, knowledge of the individual and the care requirements without these key needs the individuals care may not be met and illness, isolation and poor standards could happen. The main aim of partnership working is the well being of the service users ensuring they have the services and needs required by groups of individuals and building relationships to maintain the well being.

1.4

There are many barriers to good partnership working these include, services although having the clients care needs in hand they will always prioritise their treatments and requirements first due to their beliefs its importance outweighs other aspects. Day to day commitments can alter due to needs of others within the service and can impede on the service requirements of some we look after. Poor planning and lack of communication are barriers usually thrust upon our service by others and we have to alter plans and commitments to fulfil the needs.

We overcome barriers in our setting by training and supervising staff to a good level, have good communication skills and consistently share information and knowledge which allows for any staff member to fill in roles that require attention. We employ a diverse staff group with different beliefs that do not hinder the care needs of those we support.

We are the main care givers and will be the coordinators within the care team to centralise all needs from service users, families and professionals. We have to prioritise the care needs of those we look after making sure that the importance of what needs to be done from the service users standpoint and ours is completed first. Within our setting we have good relationships with everyone and are usually left to define the importance of the client's needs. We have regular activities and monthly activity planners for all service users and keep a diary of day to day needs for the service users we look after, this will allow us to plan days and request extra staffing if required for the days. We have delegated responsibilities, keyworkers and team hierarchy which all contribute to overcoming the barriers and perform an affective service.

2 Be able to establish and maintain working relationships with Colleagues.

My role and responsibilities in working with colleagues are: empowering those I support and work with, training and supervising those I work with to improve skills and knowledge and improve the care given to those we support. Working in partnership with the manager, area manager and head office to deliver a dignified person centred qualified and quality service.

We all work together with the aim to provide the best care possible for those we support complimenting each other by using strengths and identifying weaknesses of everybody we work with. We will have regular appraisals, which is a yearly reflection on how we believe we are performing our strengths and weaknesses and what we have and want to achieve. I complete supervisions on staff on many aspects of care giving again identifying areas which people perform strongly or need assistance with, this evaluates the performance. I complete AAA assessments yearly on staff giving a brief self reflection then management perspective on attitude, attendance and ability. My role is also a trainer and mentor so I actually train 4 different aspects of care which I have been trained to do, help on other areas of training and support staff in development of skills and ability.

We have keyworkers who are responsible for the care planning updates and day to day needs of the service user, I would be the liaison between the staff and manager obtaining information making sure things get recorded and activities and appointments get booked and then are achieved.

I report directly to my manager with any integral information having to decipher what is required to be passed on to both above and below me to make sure we have a smooth running service. Resolving conflicts that could arise with service users or colleagues and keeping a happy service. I have to be flexible and help my colleagues be flexible by training everyone to a high standard which permits inter unit working and better knowledge by all staff involved. Working together in these ways help benefit the people we support and the organisation in providing a quality service.

I chair regular monthly team meetings which allow for home issues and agendas to be transmitted throughout the colleague group. This also allows for my colleagues to transmit any issues or support they want.

2.2, 2.3 & 2.4

To develop common objectives and deliver better working practices with colleagues we must utilise the staff group identify the strengths of everyone and get them involved in the development of care delivery. This will obviously depend on the vulnerability of the service user and the complexity of their needs because the support level and need will vary. We have to promote responsibility in the workforce however keeping accountability. The nature of the care home is that ultimately the manager is accountable for everything in the care home but if they were to have to complete or micro manage every task then the home and care standards would fall or not be accomplished. A good manager is only as good as the workforce beneath them, having trained quality assistant manager or seniors to be accountable to the managers and staff teams accountable to the seniors. Training and supervising staff to obtain a workforce that is reliable, quality and accountable for all aspects in the homes care standards.

We must look at the individuals their competency and ability balance it with their attitude and within the working environment adapt and use experience and strengths to deliver a person centred care programme for those we look after. Working together builds relationships, delivers integration and hopefully integrity throughout the workforce, utilising skills and attributes for the common goal. There is investment of both time and money through training and development of the staff group which is mutually beneficial.

My working relationship with colleagues is a mixture of promoting the best out of my staff and utilising their strengths. Knowing the strengths and benefits of individuals can access different ideas and viewpoints understanding different cultures and beliefs. Different knowledge and backgrounds from staff can help bridge gaps in both knowledge and care quality of residents. With any relationship there has to be boundaries these are there to protect everyone and both improve and ensure quality care. My role is senior to those I supervise and although everyone is accountable for their own actions being senior makes me more accountable for the homes running, residents and staff. Ensuring a professional relationship and following the company's policies and procedures keeps the needs of those I supervise and support balanced and effective.

In every work environment there is conflict from time to time, managing the conflict and constructively dealing with it is the necessity. Roles in care can become blurred this has its perks as we overlap care practices and ultimately give a more joined together service. Although lines can be blurred we have to maintain distinct roles as well this helps manage conflicts because we can say that this is actually mine or your responsibility and complete tasks as needed. We may have to look at disciplinary and at this point our roles are set I am the boss you the worker this is complying with policies and procedures and allows for effective working practice. Conflict can arise over anything and we have to be mindful of accountability, making sure that what we do is in best interest and correct with a trail following guidelines so as if something occurs we can answer why we did it even if technically not our jobs. With any conflict we have to be balanced in our approach and see all angles so as to resolve any issues.

3 Be able to establish and maintain working relationships with other professionals.

Looking at my own role and responsibilities in relation to other professionals, my role is front line I support individuals I look after every day liaising with other bodies to accommodate and promote the service users welfare, health, wishes and beliefs.

Every person in the service users care package should be safeguarding the individual from harm and abuse while balancing their rights and interest to promote health and wellbeing.

Everybody should be respecting client's wishes and choices as long as we give informed choice and balance risk management.

My role is to ensure the day to day needs of the individual are met. We support the individual through all aspects of their life like health; this can be supplying and making nutritional meals and drinks throughout the day to support client's diet. If required we would help access dieticians to assist by being primary carer we have more knowledge and the day to day support package to help achieve any goals. Activities such as gym for clients wishing to attend would be sourced and choices given to clients, support would be offered to those that required it. Accessing treatments for physical ailments is an important aspect of my job for our service users giving choices on services available. Some service users I have are fully independent and make their own appointments for any treatments just giving us prescriptions to order from our pharmacy. Other service users require us to book appointments and attend appointments with them also collecting medicines from pharmacy.

Supporting individuals as we do requires knowledge of the clients their likes, dislikes, needs and requirements. We liaise with them or for them with many different services our responsibility as primary carer is to put client first in their care needs, assist with care delivery and help communication between services, bridging gaps from clients to professionals recorded all outcomes and centralising the clients care.

Professionals are all different have different expertise and will prioritise their service before anyone else's. Language used by some professionals is not necessary language that our clients understand so at times we become intermediates deciphering the information and transferring to the client.

When communicating with professionals we must always think about the client and what is best for them sometimes this is not always what a professional wants but might be the need or wish or client. Within all services we have common practices, policies and procedures this includes identifying and challenging discrimination.

Communication is very important, knowing when to listen or speak. Communicate using facts or beliefs they all play an aspect we have to negotiate what the clients want and our aims for service user I said previously sometimes that what can be wanted may not be what's offered so we have to compromise.

Respect everyone we all have jobs to do, no one person can manage everything required in a person's care package we delegate and we assist, completing the best care package for the individual together as a team with the mutual goal of the health, wellbeing and social needs of those we are fortunate to assist.

3.2

Having strong partnerships helps deliver the best care package for the individuals we support. Having a relationship that is factual, open, honest and sensible is essential for this. There are many aspects we have to look at in any relationship in care, it can be data sharing protected by the data protection act which allows for information sharing on a need to know basis, this is also an essential aspect of partnership working sharing information that is relevant and needed instead of the information that is not required by that certain individual. The other main aspect to look at is the individual, making sure that the person receives the care that is required and is in a format understood by the client themselves. There are risks involved in partnership working that the client's needs can be neglected or not fully met because different services are obtained from different sources, this is why the primary carer will centralise the information and produce communication lines between services and clients so the client doesn't get marginalised and forgotten.

The home I work for have always worked productively within the health and social care sector building good relationships and optimising communications. Keeping the team appraised of any situations through fax, email, phone and face to face meetings (both on a professional level or a more relaxed conversation) is one of our most basic procedures. Many services we deal with will leave the day to day aspects of the clients care with us unless we express a need for input. Then being contacted on a regular basis for check-ups and meetings to review the client's package. We have always contacted the relevant services whether GP, consultant, CPN or social worker with any information about the client that they are responsible for and we need the assistance for.

3.3, 3.4 & 3.5

One of the main ways we ensure common goals and principles while looking after individuals is meetings such as CPA care program approach or CHC community health care assessments. These will help look at the individual from both health and social needs including the client, support team (carers and family), health team and social team into the meeting. The assessment would look at all aspects of the care plan, have feedback from teams and identify any risks or requirements. Anything that is identified will be asked to be completed by an appointed individual or team with desired outcome to be obtained under a time period agreed using the smart principle. The desire of having meetings is that all people in the care circle of the individual can put their views across gets listened to and has a response to the query. Ultimately the team meet with the individual or on behalf if declined to meet but always with that person at the centre of decision making process. We use meetings as a tool to benefit from everyone's experience being able to establish what's working and not also identifying the different team's objectives and what is beneficial or disadvantaged to everyone and compromising for the service users need. When looking at any objectives we have to prioritise and agree the outcomes that is being requested being specific and inclusive.

Having the regular meetings allows for evaluating of what has been agreed and can measure the effectiveness of the partnership by being able to review and reflect directly from last meeting and to access whether objectives were met. We can learn from our mistakes and successes to better accomplish partnership working in future building on previous experiences. Within our own workplace we carry out appraisals yearly and supervisions every month and as much training as is available. We monitor, record and deal with and complaints and compliments every time they arise and complete monthly audits on this and other aspects of the home. Every year we get assessed by outside agencies such social services contract monitoring and CQC who are both independent and investigate our service for compliance and quality. These can be accessed by anyone looking to enter our home or be placed here. The inspections will show if any improvements are required for the service.

We can only control the homes agendas policies and procedures and try to improve care with support from other agencies and professionals if we find that the support is not being received even when asked for we will inform CQC as the duty of care to clients may not be being met from the other teams.

As with any partnership conflicts will arise on both practice and what is perceived as being the best outcome. Successfully distinguishing between control and influence is a great way to overcome such barriers. Within the care sector no one body will have control over the individuals care needs but may ascertain more power than others, for example a doctor will take lead on physical health which will prioritise over everything else however mental health teams and carers will input to this situation but the doctor will have more control due to the qualified nature of his job and the wellbeing of the client. This does not mean control however because other factors have to be taken into account as well as the individual themselves. So influence is really the power having leadership skills and being able to sensitively deal with situations arising for the client could change that the carers will have the influence to change the outcome. Example a doctor may believe a client requires to go to hospital for treatment but the carers suggest that treatment could be carried out at home with some intervention from outpatient teams, this may not be as intrusive and may not have such a negative effect on client's mental wellbeing. Given these perimeters a doctor may reassess his verdict and opt for this other option. Partnership working can only successfully be achieved with give and take from all involved managing any confrontation as and when it arises looking for the best interest and outcome for the service user.

4 Be able to work in partnership with others.

4.1

1997 saw the biggest leap into inter agency partnership working, prior to this different agencies for health and social care would work independently which would lead to increased delays and possible unsatisfactory outcomes for those using services. When the government changed the health act and introduced the inter agency policy it was perceived as a lot of work with confusion as well. People were reluctant in this new principle sharing their knowledge and expertise with everyone, the belief was things wouldn't be as effective and teams would be downgraded and decisions would take longer to make, giving poor care to those being looked after.

This opinion these negative views were narrow minded, it was more preservation than caring for others

Today partnership working is operating well it does have a few faults where individuals cant share information but overall is one of the best policies for public care of the 20th century.

Working together to achieve a common goal of better health and social care for those requiring it is very important. Barriers are broken providing greater data sharing centralising information about a client and enabling care to be given from health services and have social contribute when they are required in the care process. This streamlines the care system frees up beds and services in the hospitals and provides support in community homes and hospices for those needing support.

The individuals needing care should receive continuous support for their needs both in service and out in the community. The level of support can change and adapt to the individuals current levels of support need with 24hr support and communication from all aspects of the clients care team. Teams can learn and develop of each other skills and training in the health and social care field learning from errors and good practice. Developing a better overall service for all that use this sector. Voluntary groups and advocates have made a leap forward in this sector helping assist in areas that have lacked or were not there previously addressed, these put a new dynamic on health and social care because of the independence of the voluntary sector new ideas and practices were brought along bringing a better support level for those they assisted. Questions were asked and a need to comply were made as these groups worked for the client and their best interest looking after their human rights. Partnership working is an organic machine a living breathing organism that is forever changing to better itself, adapting through trainings, legal proceedings and good practice with the goal of promoting wellness and inclusion.

4.2

Outcomes framework for adult's social services (DOH 2011) details four domains for development in future services.

1. Enhance quality of life for people with care and support needs.
2. Delaying and reducing the need for care and support.
3. Ensure people have a positive experience of care and support.
4. Safeguarding the vulnerable in these circumstances and protecting them from avoidable harm.

The health and social care sector are asked to work in partnership with service user and carers to develop the care requirement, there is an understanding that some people don't want to contribute in their care needs and the provider will have to manage the care needs in best interest. There is also a need for service users to have greater knowledge and understanding of their rights and needs so advocates can work on the client's behalf to help them gain the knowledge and understanding to obtain what they should receive.

The framework for adults suggest to give support to those that really need it at the point that is appropriate, making sure the support is of a good standard, protecting clients from avoidable harm and enhancing their quality of life.

Working together from initial assessment and need of care support, to reviews on treatments and level of support required using a dynamic approach allows for a quality working practice that's effective in the field.

Each company will have its own personal policies and procedures that they follow, in partnership we follow government laws and legislation trying to work for the best interest of the clients.

4.3

Working in partnership requires all agencies to have a common objective, primary objective is the best care and support for the individual they are looking after. There will be many other objectives all based in promoted wellbeing, health and happiness. No two individuals will have the same objectives in their care needs because everyone is different that is why the care industry is designed as being person centred, unique or tailor made for that person.

Each individual I support and care team I communicate with is different the needs are different and the requirements for the home is different. Working with agencies we all agree to policies and procedures to follow which are specific to different service users. There can become times where different agencies will contra indicate the other in service requirement and a compromise needs to be agreed so we all work the same.

Identifying who is the lead and who is accountable for different aspects of care are essential for partnership working. Within Leicestershire there are many different training bodies training the same qualifications, we use the NHS and county council for a lot of our training, as well as training in home that follows a nationally recognised training system. These all allow us to develop the staff team and promote and provide a uniformed approach to basic care.

4.4

The best way we can evaluate the care in our homes is by agencies inspecting us. Our own company completes regular yearly monitoring looking at bed stats, costs, staff turnover finances to name a few.

Social services contracts monitoring visit every year, they will inspect the care given, staff efficiency, compliance of their policies, value for money and the flexibility of the care and workforce.

Maggie Lewin our contracts monitor will speak to both staff and residents privately to assess their opinions on the service and the knowledge they have. She will look at care plans randomly to assess the relevance and accuracy of details and that they are updated daily with current situations and day to day occurrences. Two staff files are also took at random and assessed to ascertain staffs ability and knowledge. Other documents are seen by Maggie they include, maintenance book, fire book, meds book, audits folder, quality matters file also staff rotas for the last month.

Maggie completes a thorough inspection of all files and documents to assess our compliance and competence, making sure the home is suitable and relevant for the county occupants.

After inspection feedback is given our last inspection two weeks ago was said we were compliant in all areas and that they are pleased with our service. We are still awaiting written documents on report.

CQC will carry out a similar inspection usually yearly or two yearly due to last report.

Both agencies have powers, these start with compliance measures but could end up with lost contracts, closure or even legal proceedings.

When we look inside ourselves we can become complacent and blind sighted, this to us is why we rely on the agencies to help us identify shortfalls or even quality so we can provide the care required having guidance and feedback.

4.5

Conflict in care management arises quite often managing conflict then becomes an essential aspect of care. Tensions usually arise when certain services believe they are being dumped on or not listened to. This is why we must have clear policies and procedures to follow in any event of a person's care. We must utilise the CPA and clients care plan to establish boundaries and procedures to follow in the event something occurs. The agencies have then got to react and respond in accordance with these agreed policies. When people work the way they should it removes the strain on other services to the more trained individuals. Also giving the care they need at that time. Police services will often say they feel burdened with mental health, this is because the funding is not available to accommodate everyone. In the past ten years I have noticed an influx of people being downgraded in their care needs, those that need secure are in semi secure, those from semi move to low, those in low move to homes like ours, and then clients who should be with us move to the community, in the community care lapses again in support levels, this then requires police intervention and inevitable that person re-enters care setting at higher level than should be just because the funding was not available to assist before they got ill.

Unfortunately the finance is not available in this sector to accommodate everyone, the care is better and is working well considering all the changes occurring over recent years, teams have progressed and adapted quickly to provide quality service. The main aspect is that those that are in the service must have the care required in the good times and the bad, the extra assistance needs accessing quickly and the teams to follow the CPA designed without this we are failing the clients. This does still arise now where we are told we have to wait for the client to fail before services can react this is a negative response to what should be a proactive service not a reactive service.

CU2941 Use and Develop Systems that Promote Communication

1 1.1 Be able to address the range of communication requirements in own role.

In my job role I communicate with many different people on a day to day basis, each individual may have different communication needs and understand information in different ways. Some of the key aspects of communication in my role is being open and honest, being approachable and then being able to decipher the information given to me and respond appropriately asking questions when required to gather further information. Having the ability to listen to people is one aspect but communicating back is another. Making sure what is said is appropriate for the audience, informative and factual.

In my role I communicate with service users that have mental health and/or learning disabilities my approach would be to talk directly to client using simple understandable language, making sure that the client understands what is said by repeating info in a brief summary, I know giving to much information could confuse my clients so keeping it short is a key point. Service users will communicate to me their needs and this may not be coherent information or really what they want to say, I have to take my time with clients and ask questions, repeat back what is said at times we have to read between lines and propose what they mean as some clients will not say what they really mean.

Service users family is treated much the same, some have a good understanding of illnesses and we can talk more in depth, however some do not understand so we again break down the information given to a more understandable level. Much the same as service users listening to family can be a tricky time because again we have to decipher what they say to the information or advise they are looking for. With family we have to be careful because our service users have the right to confidentially and may not want their families to know what is going on so we respect their choice unless deemed that the information does need sharing in the best interest of our clients.

Communication with staff and colleagues can take many forms from verbal communication one to one or group discussions, we could give handouts, letters or books that the staff needs to know. There is key information that needs passing on and we must make sure that all staff understands what is meant so using long words and jargon may get lost in translation, so again keeping the context easy to understand and asking questions is encouraged to demonstrate the understanding.

Professionals are the other people we communicate with daily whether it be GP's, nurses, cpn's, social workers, consultants or other agencies like cqc or council services. This group of people prefer information being directed with just factual information because of time restraints and need to understand basics without the extra information. This is our job to decide what is factual and is needed to know and what is generally irrelevant to this sector. We again have to understand what is said to us from the professionals, keeping notes of meetings or conversations is good as we can refer back to this information if and when required.

1.2

Being able to support the individuals we care for with the best level of care means that prior to admission to our service we assess the individual. Assessing their communication along with many other aspects, this allows us to know whether we could provide the support required. Some cases would require staff to have further training like makaton to support those that couldn't verbally communicate but knew sign language. Other method of communication are verbal, written, sign and audio communication. Some service users may have poor communication in any area and may require specialist services or agencies like SALT to help with the communication needs. Regardless of communication or even intellect we would speak slowly, clearly and factually summarising what has been said. On admission we complete a communication care plan this allows staff to know best ways to support the individual but also allows us to check for change in the future. When admitted all service users are presented with a welcome pack and a tour of the home. The welcome pack includes the complaints procedure which is also verbally expressed to the client so client knows how to receive the best service possible. We also display a complaints procedure in each unit and the reception area. Staff are to make themselves available at all times for clients so if they want anything staff are there. We also have monthly residents meetings so clients can bring up anything they want to. Staff undergo many training courses that include communication, record and report writing and safeguarding these give staff the knowledge on how best to support service users in day to day communication and in whistleblowing on abuse. Clients again may come from different backgrounds and as a service we would aim to deliver a service for everyone and every background even if meant learning languages. As a service we communicate with many outside agencies like cqc and council aswell as cpn and social worker's and is our responsibility to make sure we keep accurate up to date information and pass on the information when required. Staff are trained well in our workplace in many different aspects including communication and they understand that what is said by an individual is only 10% of what is actually said, the tone of voice body language and expression make up the rest of what is said, so staff need to look and listen when communicating also making sure they take notice how they deliver their communication making sure what is said marries up to how we say it.

1.3 & 1.4

In our home there are many barriers to communication due to our clientele, our main service users have mental health or learning disabilities which could impair the understanding of the information. Depression, anxiety, disability, behaviour, and self esteem are but a few barriers that are directly from service users illnesses, overcoming these can be hard, staff would under go training to understand better the conditions like depression, mental health, learning disabilities and antisocial behaviour. Once completed training staff would understand better the conditions and ways to communicate, taking time, talking calmly and none threatening are a few ways to overcome the barriers but ultimately the clients have to be willing to communicate in some way otherwise no amount of training can help.

Other barriers we see in home is the environment, lighting, heating, seating, cleanliness and noise. Without alienating anyone we have to try and promote a safe versatile home. Communal areas will tend to be calming colours with pictures to break up big block colours. The lighting will be on and heating set to a comfortable level, this won't please everyone but unfortunately the needs of the many outweigh the needs of the few. Private rooms can be more colourful and unique allowing for lighting changes and heat changes to suit individuals better. Seating in our home promotes openness with sofas on edges of rooms and then dining table in middle for closure more personal activities and feeding. Noise again in the communal areas are tried to be kept lower so to encourage people to communicate, in clients room they play music and TV louder but we still ask clients to respect each other and minimise noise at times.

Having assumptions about people is negative communication due to someone being female/ male, gay/ straight or Christian/Muslim doesn't mean they are what we have as a preconceived stereotype everyone is different and unique and are treated as so, if we treat people on assumptions then the care the person gets may not be right for them and we could be breaking the law, also clients would become dissatisfied with the service and could withdraw or harm themselves, certainly trust wouldn't be able to be built. Same as having authority over someone influencing behaviours and ways people feel they have to communicate. These are all barriers we have to adapt be open and be approachable at all times so to alleviate the barriers.

1.5

Words are power; they allow us to express our wants and needs, allows expressing happiness, pain, discomfort and empower us to make choices. Expressing ourselves through communication allows individuals to have a person centred care package all about how best to support the person, needs, likes, dislikes etc.

Verbal communication is the main source of communication in the world however the way and demeanour of how we say things probably means more than the words themselves. E.g., the words "its alright take your time no rush" states one thing but couple it with shouting the words, encroaching on peoples space, taping watch or folded arms changes the context of the words and shows the person listening that actually we are in a rush.

We have to watch body language and tone because if not matching to words it can become confusing. The language we use is also important jargon, slang or complex words may not be understood. We have to be clear, concise, use appropriate language and body language for people to actually know what we mean.

Other communications methods are lip reading, makaton, writing, pictures and touch. All these communication methods get used all round the world daily it allows everybody a way of expressing themselves which allows them to get what they need or want.

2 Be able to improve communication systems and practices that support positive outcomes for individuals

2.1 & 2.2

In our homes we have many different systems and practises for communication.

1. Communication care plan, this is documented straight away on introduction to our service. It shows how the person communicates and what support is required in this area, this will be reviewed every year or sooner if required. This is our baseline on admission and allows us to be able to check for change further down the line. Initial assessments can be thin for information as our clients can take a long time to get to know and information to be available. The assessment is good because its one sheet in the care plan just about communication that summarises the needs.
2. Daily reports, one to one, these are documented each day and can inform us of any needs asociated or changes occurred that day. These may not be as informative as we would like and information written down is completed by one person and may not reflect all the information from the day. Daily reports are good to demonstrate how things change daily and allow a larger picture to develop for the persons care.
3. Health action plans, these are more in-depth person centred plans mainly focused around a person's health requirements, these should include a lot of information of how the client is what they need, like and how best to communicate with the individual. These are a great source of information when used correctly but people tend to overlook these and just fill in the ordinary care plans. The other downfall is that the health action plans were designed for people with learning disabilities only.

4. Daily handovers and handover sheets, the handovers occur at the end of each shift and allows for the information of the day to be passed onto the next shift coming on. These are one of the most commonly used methods of information sharing in the industry it allows the information to be passed on in a brief informative manor. The weak point seems to me that staff get tired at end of shift and forgets partial information and misses it from handover or the information given can be irrelevant instead of the facts required. So handover books in each unit get filled out during day. So as things occur they get documented and between the two methods all information should be handed over effectively.
5. Weekly handover meeting, this is similar to the daily handover but communicates the information of the midweek shifts to the weekend team, at the same time it allows any other relevant information to be passed on.
6. Senior handover, at the end of each shift pattern the seniors and manager speak by phone and communicate the information that has occurred on shift, this will be for the whole home and allows for certain personal information to be passed on that the other staff do not need to know. Due to the senior not being on individual floors they rely on their team to inform them of what's occurred so they can handover however information can be missed, handover generally takes place an hour or so before end of shift so we could miss vital details at end of shift so would need to pass on through night staff.
7. Monthly meetings, this allows for all comments queries and information to be passed on to all staff and keeps the service up to date with any changes to the service and requirements. The meeting notes get wrote up and displayed for all staff to read and sign to say they understand what has been said. Some staff however do not read the information or attend meetings which could cause problems for the service, once signed however it is a legal document and if staff go against what is said will be used in disciplinary action of staff.

All of our meetings and handovers are conducted behind closed door in the best attempt to keep all information private and confidential as directed in the data protection act. Care plans are locked away in the office and information will be shared with appropriate people only. We keep records of handover sheets and meetings and produce these to cqc and council services to evidence the care and information exchange.

2.3

Our team meetings monthly would have a small agenda but ended up growing during the meeting, they wouldn't always follow the path originally designed. The senior team sat down and spoke of the best way to improve meetings and allow the information to flow. We came up with a few ideas we have decided to hand out the meeting dates for the entire year so all staff can make themselves available for the meetings. We also started writing the meeting notes before the meeting so we were clear about the meeting and followed the guide without detouring. We always allow for a round robin were any staff member can comment what they would like. Doing the above has allowed for an easier meeting with all concerns being addressed in a timely manner. We will then print of a complete meeting notes and pin on board all staff are observed reading and signing document. Once all staff have completed we put into audit file ready for any inspections, this also allows us to re visit the previous meetings quickly and easily if discrepancies occur.

2.4

We have many different organisational points in the home, delegated responsibilities which is a list of jobs that staff are responsible to complete daily, weekly or monthly. We have a keyworker list which shows who should be in charge of monthly evaluation and the care plan of clients. We have audits lists which show when things should be updated and by whom. We follow supervisions, appraisals and training guides to make sure staff has the knowledge and feedback required to complete their jobs well. These can be discussed at meetings every month so documented and signed by staff, handouts can be given and displayed so everyone knows what is required. We have private discussions with staff on a one to one basis allowing for privacy and openness without the feeling of being singled out or picked on. We often check that the work has been carried out by the individuals and to a good standard. We will often reflect back on how someone's doing and if it could be improved, this can be as often as daily but usually every 6 months. Staff are encouraged to speak openly and honestly airing grievances in private so we can resolve issues and provide a top quality service.

3 Be able to improve communication systems to support partnership working

In our workplace all of our service users care plan front sheets are computerised, all other information on clients is handwritten and stored in the care folder, these are locked away in the office for data protection which will only be assessed by staff, these will be shared to relevant people according to data protection act during meetings concerning individual clients. Also being open to organisations who monitor our service like cqc and Leicestershire council. Staff files are open to these agencies as well but are not shared to anyone else without permission. When required information needs to be taken doctors etc we photocopy relevant sheets and take with us. On occasion we scan, fax and or email them to relevant services. The information held at the home can be viewed by the service user at any time and if expressed shared with family and friends but only if agreed by client.

Documents that are relating to service user which is multi agency will be displayed in care plan and will be property of client, if the client moves home this information will leave with them to new service, however PLs paperwork i.e. daily reports and records are property of PL and remain behind. They will be kept and stored for the time required by law under the data protection act.

Not everyone is privy to certain information for example a chiropodist would not need to know medication, but would need to know if on a blood thinner due to risks. A diabetic nurse would need info on diet, weight, chiropody, eyes etc but wouldn't need information regarding mental health unless it affects that care aspect.

Being a care manager or senior for the individual we are centre point and require all information to be able to give best service needed however we are not privy to medical records even though we get shared information.

Computerising all of our records could stream line the data sharing between homes but runs a huge risk of poor data protection as all information would be available to everyone in the care path associated with the service user as daily reports and one to one sheets cover many topics. This also leaves us open to data loss or changing which is illegal and bad practise. Also the obvious hacking.

Written documents however could get lost or destroyed, they become bulky and harder to search through for information, but a hard copy becomes more difficult to alter or replicated without questioning authenticity due to signatures etc.

Both forms of recording have the same issue if not recorded and updated regular they are useless and can be misunderstood so mistakes occur which could result in injury, illness, poor service or even death.

All communications with care team in the home is documented and any activities etc are all documented, this allows for a complete care plan that effectively allows for the service users needs to be evaluated and needs to be met.

Sharing information between services allows the best possible care package for service user and allows for better and quicker support available when required. This also gives consistent care throughout services.

One way I can see improvement would be a national database with assess restriction under job description, with information tagging software, so keyword search would bring up any relevant information about service users to word definition, for example a dietician could assess records relating to physical health and eating and drinking records using a keyword search of diet.

Regular team meetings with agencies like cqc or social services with their own systems and requirements should happen yearly with all managers in locations, with topics sent ahead so any queries could be discussed at meeting. There must also be a system put in place so all governmental agencies and cqc work with same standards because currently standards required can differ and confuse services of actual requirements needed for the service users.

In any meeting we have, information gets passed on from both sides some can conflict so at this point a compromise has to occur to find an adequate solution to problem. After all the service users' best interest and welfare is priority so listening to all ideas and having an agreed solution is what's needed. Sometimes like with daycentres timetables and a handover sheet would be the agreed way of working to handover appropriate information.

4 Be able to use systems for effective information management

In the care industry it can become hard to determine at times whether data should be shared or not. It is an esthetical dilemma when the law says we should respect people's privacy.

The human rights act article 8 states individuals have the right to respect for their private life (scie.org)

However this is not an absolute right and it can be overridden if necessary and in accordance with the law. This mainly comes down to safeguarding and I suppose in a sense the right to life.

The data protection act will also say that as long as the information is necessary for the purpose which it is being shared, but can only be shared with those who have a need for it, it must be accurate and up to date, also shared securely and not kept for any longer than is required. (scie.org)

Individuals can ask for people not to know information or may ask us to keep it private, we have to determine the seriousness of the information given and ask will it have a detrimental effect if shared or not. For example if someone disclosed they were having problems going toilet and we were asked not to tell anyone we would talk to them and ask them to see doctor we would record all said and tell those in charge of care, if the person refused to go doctors we would monitor the individual, however when the service user declines physically we have to break data protection to ensure the service user gets the medical attention they need this protects them and ourselves and is safeguarding.

A client may make a disclosure to a staff member and ask for it not to be shared but we have a duty of care to the individual to inform police etc if needed, which we would tell client, this can destroy a relationship that the staff have with client even though it's in the best interest.

This is where the ethically dilemma is because our job is build good relationships with those we look after, however a allegation of abuse would mean we have to break trust even though we keep it as private as possible. The legal aspect takes over safeguarding, protection and duty of care we must disclose this information or we become an abuser ourselves. Determining whom it should be shared with is where the data protection comes in because not everyone needs to know only those pertinent to care, investigation and decision making.

To determine whether information should be shared we use a generic tool which is called the Caldecott principles (scie.org) this means we should

Justify the purpose for why the information is needed

Only use personally identifiable information when absolutely necessary

Use the minimum personal identifiable information possible

Access to the information should strictly be need to know.

Everyone should be aware of their roles in respect to confidentiality.

Understand and comply with law in data protection act, police and criminal evidence act and human rights act.

So firstly we must ask is the information really needed for the purpose we are using it for, for example a disclosure that one service user hit another person within service would mean police involvement for assault. So things like photos, incident reports and statements would be shared also in our service clients diagnoses will be shared due to nature of industry. Things like what they eat, how often they wash etc would not because it's not pertinent.

Only using personal information like names when required this would be to police, hospitals because they need the name of client to be exact and true, however in incident reports we would use initials because these could be shared amongst different service user's teams and the details of the other service user is not required. For places like cqc we would use a unique identifier code which is sent to them but we keep a key to who's who in a file so can be checked if necessary.

Information should be on a need to know basis so for instance a chiropodist doesn't need to know any information unless it affects them like diabetes, a serious transferable illness or being on blood thinners.

Everyone within our home on employment gets instructed on the data protection act and safeguarding etc and then gets informed in home how we promote data protection. There are no discussions of clients in the open areas, or out of work, we must keep all records private safe and secure failure to do so will result in termination and possible legal proceedings.

Each staff member undergoes training in the standards which is in the first 12 weeks of employment this covers what we should do in case of abuse, data protection and the human rights. We also undergo many other trainings like safeguarding, mca/dols which instruct us of our responsibilities. If and when there are amendments to the law the staff are notified by letter and are requested to sign to say they understand the amendments.

We manage our information systems by keeping all service users personal data locked in a secure office. When completed information in care plans we do this in private so as no clients or others see information on service users. We keep some computerised records which only the three senior staff has access to by password. Information will be shared to those relevant to individuals care. This is usually consultants, cpns and social workers; they will also be open to inspection by cqc or social services. Clients have a right at any time to see all information on them again we promote it being viewed in a secure way. We sit with clients and speak about their care to fill in information in care plans, at times they will not agree with what we say so we discuss the reasoning behind what we say, they still may not agree but we are factual to the knowledge and evidence we have in front of us. We follow PLs policy of data handling which all staff read and sign acknowledgement. (See attached)

CU2942 Promote Professional Development

1 Understand principles of professional development.

Globally in the last thirty years there have been huge leaps forward in every industry including the health care sector. People are looking for and demanding a better service with higher expectations of care sought after. Due to new legislations, research, government policies, initiatives, guidance and inquiry findings the care industry changes with more frequency than ever before.

Due to the higher demand on better health care staff constantly undergo new training or receives updates on current training. To go along with training, policies and procedures change and all staff must be aware of these changes as out of date information could result in a poor service given or illegal practices being undertaken.

Staff initially undertakes training in the Standards of practice training which were seven sections outlining aspects in safeguarding, dignity in care etc however these have now changed and there are 10 initial training aspects to look at in the twelve week probation period. As a home we prioritise health and safety and safeguarding. Staff will then attend safeguard training and medication training. We currently attend around 50 different training courses/ papers in the home. The key trainings pertinent to our home are actively sourced and undertook as needed, the extra trainings we attend when they are available within our locations. We also partake in brief trainings called 60 seconds which cover a great deal of the care industry as well as regular supervisions. Aspects of care can change rapidly so staff will undertake regular training in the key areas of care like safeguarding, moving and handling and first aid. We monitor the training through a training matrix one developed by our head office and one done by myself which is more comprehensive. When the laws change or policies are altered we are immediately advised by our head office so staff can be informed of changes and if needed training to be re-sat with the alterations. It's our job to explain these changes to staff and make sure they understand the changes and are trained to the new standards.

If staff are not informed of changes and don't receive regular training even those that they have done before staff become out of date and the care given to our clients could put them at risk. The home could become liable to law suits or could even close due to guidelines not being met. Staff often believe because they have trained in an area before that they know the information but because of the fast growth in health care sector in becomes outdated and useless. Then in some circumstances new staff to the home will be trained wrong because they have the wrong information passed to them.

We believe that having regular updates and meetings to discuss new directives help us achieve the best possible service for our clients.

2 & 3

In training there seems to be many barriers firstly people's ability/ attitude to learn.

People may struggle with learning have poor written communication or understanding of the information, this will put people off or sit in training and not be getting the information required. We can try to alleviate this by having different training styles.

Some staff work nights so would not be available the days that training occurs; we can try to look at different days and or times to suit night staff. Although this is not always available.

Training can occur ever while on shift which could put strain on the service and would not permit all staff to attend courses. When off shift our staff does not get paid to attend courses and this stops them wanting to attend. We can try to have several sessions of training so there is opportunity for everyone to attend and PL should pay the staff for attending the courses.

Lack of resources in vicinity, again staff have to make their own way to training so anything too far away will stop people attending, staff again do not get paid for transportation costs, if our head office paid staff to attend and/ or tried to source training nearer to home staff may become more willing to attend sessions.

Culture/ beliefs can play a part in having barriers in training due to personal feelings that this is not acceptable for them to attend. Against religious beliefs etc.

There are many different training methods:

One to one this is personal between trainer and trainee.

Group which are two plus candidates

Supervisions which are when a senior staff member oversees a staff member undertake a task they will observe and give feedback on the supervision.

Reading this could just be simply reading a passage of text that outlines or updates a training aspect.

Visual training is when you tend to watch a clip or presentation on aspect of training.

Aural tends to be like a seminar when someone stands there talking about the training.

There is also kinaesthetic learning which leans towards tactile learning so actually doing a task.

Everyone will learn differently and all the above training has merits in different ways. So in my opinion as a trainer I like to involve all styles of training to get the information across and if done right it will keep training interesting and informative, with every staff member understanding most aspects. Then when they get stuck the staff group feel more confident to ask questions without being singled out because they may excel in some styles and lack in others.

The other aspect of learning we undertake is appraisals which is a yearly sit down to express job quality and satisfaction it allows both staff and managers to find out how well they are doing and how to improve skills, also highlighting any short comings.

We have internal trainers and mentors, external agencies and nationally trained paperwork all training is good in their own way but sometimes having setting based training help the staff indentify with what is being trained.

4

When we look at training courses we look at several different aspects that could impede on training. They are:

Do we really need it – some training is not appropriate for our setting for example we would not actively search training regarding children as our service is for adults over 18.

Cost – the majority of training we look at is free council training, nhs run or training that is funded by agencies. There are circumstances we pay for training these are essential trainings like first aid where the training is required.

Commitment- there are two factors here 1. Time commitment is it a long course extending several sessions or months like qcf's. 2. The homes commitment can they release staff to attend as having the staff at the home is priority because of duty of care.

Other trainings – some training can be done through in home training or paper training rather than attending a course.

Career advancement- some staff will only want to undertake the minimum training required, where as others will do every training there is to further career and give promotion prospects.

Style – again some staff will not attend due to knowing the training would be a certain style and this puts them off, or as a home we don't believe this would be the right style of training to get the staff to gain the knowledge of the course.

Distance- staff will opt not to attend if they have to travel to training as extra costs, transportation issues and time puts them off.

Trainings also seem to overlap having to many similar training prospects on offer and we have to determine which if any is more suitable for us.

2 Be able to prioritise goals and targets for own professional development.

Evaluating your own knowledge and performance can be difficult in an evolving, growing sector. We use tools such as supervisions, appraisals and training to identify if we meet standards and benchmarks or would require further advancement in certain areas.

Training is completed as often as required it can be specific to certain aspects of our role or could be a generalised training pack. Training can be very different and could be evaluated by the trainee or the trainer also having some training that is accredited and is pass/ fail these are normally evaluated by an examination board. I believe every training that I attend I reflect on the training and ask myself questions. Was it useful? Did I learn something? Would I attend this again? And how do I implement what I learnt into my work setting?

Supervisions are again completed as often as required and focus on a specific task, they will be supervised by a senior team member, they will have adequate knowledge in this area to be able to observe assess and give feedback. These are completed on a one to one basis and could take the form of a general discussion rather than an observation. Doing supervisions allow for both supervisor and supervisee to understand where if any improvements can be made. On some occasions staff can surprise the supervisor and show them a new way of completing task that could be more service friendly. This allows for the service to develop and the team to develop with new skills.

Appraisals tend to occur on a yearly basis and are where you are able to evaluate how you believe you are doing, what improvements could be made and timescales to do so. This is usually feedback from us the appraised and feedback from the appraiser. This will include what we could do in ways of development.

AAA assessments attitude, ability and attendance again these are yearly assessment using traffic light system and comment section. So each area we grade red, amber or green and put our reasoning to the colour. The manager will then evaluate their belief to your assessment and grade you with colours and feedback. This can be a more honest way of reflection as people will generally think they are doing poorly or well but the prospective of the manager may conflict with our own.

Audits are carried out on monthly or yearly basis depending what area is being audited. We carry out our own audits and then get audited by head office or agencies. These allow for a detailed evaluation of our home and tasks. They make sure that standards are met and conformed to.

Inspections are carried out regularly by PL and outside agencies such as Leicestershire council and CQC. They look at national standards and benchmarks to how as a company and individuals we are performing. They assess every aspect of the home, care and staffing. There are always outcomes from these inspections areas to improve or new standards that need to be accomplished. They do tend to be minor changes that have occurred over the year but can make big differences. These agencies tend to give you compliance or not being strict on the principles of care. On occasion if not compliant they will schedule a repeat inspection within a set timescale where they expect you to be compliant or face sanctions, fines or closure. Although it sounds quite severe being inspected it is not actually that bad because usually you get informative feedback and ways to improve this does not mean you're not compliant just that there are a few ideas to develop your service further.

2.2

To successfully complete personal development you need to prioritise your aims and goals. Looking at several factors to help you identify these is important. We have to ask is it really required for my role? Most of the training we commit to is necessary for our role but occasionally a training opportunity arises that may not be specifically for us but we take interest anyway. So is this a priority? No not if we have other commitments that is role specific.

Would completing the training be for compliance to regulations or legislation? If yes than this is essential training and should be undertook as soon as possible. If not due to regulations or legislation than other training may take priority over this but doesn't mean you don't have to do the training it simply means it may not be the most important at that time.

Prioritising training looks at timescales when things need to be completed. Urgent training should be carried out as soon as possible this could be down to lack of skills, knowledge or compliance within the home. Less urgent training may have to be completed in longer timescales for example over the current year. Some training must be completed within a timescale of weeks, months or years due to fundings. Then some training may only arise once every so often this does not mean they are not important just not available all the time.

Our organisation will also say whether they believe it pertinent to our jobs and if not they may not fund it or allow us time off to complete. If it is required for our organisation we generally see a push of this training throughout our homes and management wanting us to attend.

One of the biggest things to look at is whether it would improve our knowledge/ skills and provide a better service for those we look after. When better service is the key in the social sector any training that improves the delivery will be a high priority usually sought after from management and will regularly trained in our homes.

3 Be able to prepare a professional development plan.

As part of a personal development plan we have to identify which is the preferred way of learning, looking at time restraints and funding options available.

Everyone has a preferred method in training some like the theory side through writing or listening, some like the observation side watching someone do something and learning from that. While others prefer a more hands on training style learning from actually doing the task. None of these are bad ways of learning as people engage differently. Most people will opt for their strength. I have a balanced training style which means I like to train using different methods and am capable of learning from any training style. As a service and manager we have to focus on our staff groups and communicate to decide how best to train staff.

Having varied training methods available is fantastic but not every subject can be trained like that so adaptation may be required so staff understand what is required.

A good plan should have the preferred way of training, timescale to when the training should be completed, and the priority of the training to do. The important thing to remember is training is required and no matter how we prefer to do the training it has to be completed. Adopting different methods for when we have time and availability is much easier than when under pressure and restraints to do so, being a good manager and helping staff may still been adapting slightly as long as we can evaluate the effectiveness and staff knowledge on subject. We also have to recognise that everyone is unique no one does the same as anyone else. We could easily alienate staff if not engaged in the training.

3.2 & 3.3

There are a few ways we develop are training plans head office have a training matrix which shows training specific to the home, on induction it is required that in the probation period that we complete the standards of care and safeguarding. After that there are other trainings that need to be completed this usually are discussed with mentor on timescales of completion. In the training files we have our own development plan which shows the training that we have completed. On our appraisals the manager will discuss any training that is required and when it should be completed by; there is then an agreement present on training required.

We have to develop a training plan using the SMART principles (specific, measurable, realistic, achievable and time-bound).

Specific training for our roles and industry, what is required and what is extra.

Measurable so having a baseline basic to work by and evaluation to see whether achieved.

Realistic it is best we look at doing things in a timely manner that is also to our level of expertise and ability. Having too much or too little training could influence quality, understanding and willingness to learn.

Achievable if we will not meet the goals set out in front of us then many people would give up. Giving an adequate time frame to quantity of work is key.

Time bound if we just say that this is the training without giving a timescale for completed then either staff will never hand it in or we would have expectations to hand in before they would be ready.

As well as the smart principles we must look at possible barriers to the learning objective and ways and means of overcoming possible barriers like a contingency plan which may have to be altered and adapted several times.

Lastly we would need to monitor and evaluate the plan again looking at timescale of monthly monitoring so as to be able to ascertain effectiveness and alterations required. This also allows us the adaptation in timescales or more required training to be put on the training plan.

Monitoring and evaluating the plan can be achieved through supervisions, appraisals and staff meetings or personal quiet time. Planning is the journey not the destination, things change and as long as we reach the final destination it does not matter which route we take.

4 Be able to improve performance through reflective practice.

Reflective practice has been around since the ancient Greeks since 500bc. Confucius said "by three methods we may learn wisdom first, by reflection, which is noblest; second, imitation, which is easiest; and third by experience which is bitterest."

Reflective practice is a tool used for self development; it has evolved over time and has many different theories. Reflective practice evolves from simple which may not have a purpose to critical which incorporates evaluation to finally critically thinking which goes further looks for reasoning/ reflection assesses and helps the individual to develop.

Personally I think the reflective process is the same for whoever wrote them just wrote in different styles.

Gibbs model asks what happened, what do you feel and think, what was good and bad and what do you make of it, then asks what else, what could change what could be done better followed by if done again what would you do differently to establish outcomes.

Kolb however has a more trial and error aspect to refection, which again is try something what was good or bad what worked what didn't and how we can alter the results.

Rolfe et al built on Bortons model asking three questions what? So what? Now what? Which again is the basic principles what has happened problem, role, what was wanted, actions taken, response and consequence. Then asks so what does it tell us what can be done to make better and what are any other issues. Now what do we do to make things better looking at the broader issues and consequences.

Dewey says we must develop a sense of the problem at hand enriching that sense with observations. Elaborating a conclusion and testing conclusion.

Reflective practice transforms a situation from obscurity, doubt or conflict into a situation that is clear and coherent.

In conclusion I would say that all models I have looked at ask the same questions of the situation what we evaluate from it and how to progress from here. Some models are more detailed but ultimately look for the same answers.

4.2, 4.3 & 4.4

The old adage of we learn from our mistakes is in essence reflective practice. In our work roles we will inevitably be in many different situations that we learn from. In no circumstance in life do we find that everything we do in one area do we repeat the same next time, that is because circumstances change life is not a machine doing the same task over and over. It is important for us to assess every situation individually on every occasion learning from previous situations. We must adapt to what is occurring at present by constantly evaluating what is happening and adjust what we do to get an outcome which is preferred. After any situation we will reflect on what occurred, what we could do next time to make things different, and record outcomes so as to allow others to see what works and doesn't work. This gives our clients a better service and our staff group better insight, training and development into practices and clients. We reflect over time because our initial judgements may be compromised by our personal beliefs or time restraints, this means we may have to reflect the next day or week, which may allow for a clearer and more efficient evaluation.

A good reflective practice would involve everyone that was present, from service users, staff or managers as we can tend to be stuck in our own judgements of situations, this could inevitably make us contribute to the problem then helping relieve the problem. We can use a tool called Joharis window, which allows for a truer more in depth evaluation by asking what is known by all, what is known to self but not others, what is known to others but not self, and the tricky one what is not known by self or others.

It takes confidence and acceptance to use this tool as some people will not want to hear negative feedback, the tool allows for training and ultimately should give better overall perspective on situation. We have to be factual, specific and have enough detail for this practise to work. Completion of such tools allows for all staff to develop learning from everyone's situations.

We don't just evaluate to improve from mistakes or failures because finding out what doesn't work is easy and improvement can be developed every time until we get the best practise required. Reflecting on what is currently working and improving from this is key because as said earlier everything can change we must adapt in every circumstance to provide best service. On occasion new techniques may arise that work better, this could cause reluctance to use as people get stuck in their ways and find change difficult. We must explore these new techniques but put into practice only if everyone understands it as this could cause more harm than good.

We must learn and adapt to new practices put forward by organisations, governmental bodies and outside agencies, this can be hard but must be done and again could take a while to adapt to the new processes and may work or not for some. Using the key elements of the new requirements we can again adapt to our own techniques through trial and error to achieve our goals.

CU2943 Champion Equality, Diversity and Inclusion

1 Understand diversity, equality and inclusion in own area of responsibility.

What is diversity, equality and inclusion? Equality is treating everybody equally and fairly regardless of ability, gender, beliefs, age, religion, race, social orientation or social status.

Diversity is recognising the differences and valuing the contribution that could be made to make an inclusive society.

Inclusion is therefore the idea that everybody has the right to be included without limitation or restriction and have a sense of belonging in life to be valued.

We have different aspects to look at within equality and diversity within our workplace. We look at staff, our policies within relation to hiring, we do not discriminate against anyone when hiring there are requirements due to health and social care practices and law like the dbs checks that may mean we don't employ someone due to barring from this sector. The general rules of will they be able to complete the job through physical or mental requirements are also looked at this is the nature of the industry as we care for others and must be able to carry out these tasks. The other aspect we look at is language unfortunately in my setting all service users speak English only so would mean that any staff member that is involved in the care practice must be able to understand and communicate in English. These restrictions may seem that we discriminate against non English speaking individuals and people who have disabilities however we actively help these individuals by looking at courses or other homes that may be more suitable with their needs.

Promotion at our organisation is based purely on ability and effort and is never discriminated against due to any gender, belief, age, social status or sexual orientation.

We value diversity as an organisation in our staff groups so people can learn new ways of doing jobs, cultural differences and can positively impact on our service users. Just like the national picture our homes is a blend of different people which means we need to actively recruit diversity to allow people to get a diverse care package.

Regarding service users we use person centred planning and or health action planning. (See appendix) this allows us to greater obtain knowledge of the people we support getting to know the likes/ dislikes and how to positively support the individual. Everyone is different and has different needs this is why we look at person centred planning because it puts the individual at the centre point of any and all decisions made about them and their care.

Prior to admission to our home we assess the individual and again have to meet certain criteria due to our service and what we can provide. We only take adults with mental health or learning disabilities as per our registration. This again sounds like discrimination but is our registration by law so is not subject to equality and diversity act.

1.2

There are many possible barriers and effects of barriers to equality and diversity within our homes and service user group. Again we can look at effects for staff and service users, in question 1 I pointed out due to our service we wouldn't employ people that are not physically, mentally or have the right language skills to our home. This is all due to the care needs of our clients and due to legal responsibilities to them we must provide a service relevant and suitable for their care. This could lead possible candidates feeling worthless or low but we as a group try to assist them into an employment in our sector which could be more appropriate for their needs.

With service users there are many barriers especially within mental health and learning disabilities that can affect the equality, diversity and inclusion that is received. Physical disabilities of those in wheelchairs could restrict movement around the home, we do have a lift, wide corridors and doors but some service users may isolate themselves due to belief it's not assessable so is our job to demonstrate and promote the assessable nature of our home.

Barriers that arise quite often are stereotyping which is when we have a preconceived idea or generalisation due to age, gender, beliefs or sexual orientation based upon our personal prejudices. This could have negative effects on the care received and could been the person is treated unfairly and end up with low self esteem, anger, isolation or lack interactions with others. A prejudice is a negative conscious or unconscious belief about groups of people for example we often hear the comments on television about Muslims harming others with bombs, subconsciously many people will feel all Muslims are the same and will actively pursue either harming them or avoiding them. This could result in our workplace with a client being abused by staff or other residents.

Discrimination occurs usually when there is a prejudice and power combined building up over time this is usually against a weaker group of individuals may be due to age, sex or race and again could result in abuse, lack of life chances, exclusion lack of personal relationships.

All these barriers could result in others also believing the prejudice and can have a major effect on how the organisation delivers care. It could cause harm to service users or staff, disempowering people and making people have low self esteem or loss of identity.

With these poor practices individuals, homes and organisations could be subject to legal proceedings took against them, people could go to jail, companies could be fined or shut down, any poor practise like this ends with negative feedback and could result with contracts being pulled from councils and also a negative review on cqc inspections. For our service user's isolation, self harm, injuries, exclusion and possible death could occur.

1.3

Legislation promotes equality, diversity and inclusion in the workplace, there are four main acts that help promote and govern this.

The disability discrimination act 1995 which now comes in the equality act 2010 which bans discrimination by employers against disabled job seekers and employees against disabled service users. The act asks employers to make reasonable adjustments for disabled people, the key word here is reasonable.

The NHS and community care act 1990 states everyone has the right to have their needs assessed by their local authority, live with dignity and independence and to avoid social isolation. The act also permits means tested funding and permits the service users to have an allowance before having to contribute towards care.

The mental health act often called sectioning is where people can be detained for treatment with or without consent for treatment. Providing the support and treatments from assessment to aftercare.

Equality act 2010 is the biggest reform to equality and discrimination of recent years; this has incorporated acts such as disability discrimination act, race discrimination act and sex discrimination act. This act legally protects people from discrimination in the workplace and wider society. Due to replacing existing laws it now becomes easier to understand and enforce, with making complaints becoming easier. It holds the basic framework to protect against discrimination and harassment. Equality act also opened up certain aspects like equal pay and not being able to hide pay scales.

These legislative practices make it easier for everybody to gain employment, be paid fairly for it and not be mistreated within the work place. Employers have to make amendments that are reasonable for disabled workers, this is positive for employees but financial could cost companies. Some employers feel that they either have to employ disabled workers or be justified not to employ them. This can cause some problems because being the most qualified for the job may not acquire the job for you as the work place may not find it reasonable to adapt the work setting enough for you to have the job.

2 Be able to champion diversity, equality and inclusion.

On employment with my employer every staff member receives a company handbook (see appendix) which outlines the companies' equality and diversity policy. Within the probation period of twelve weeks all employees are asked to read and sign the fuller policy that is in the policy folder in the office. The employees also undergo training initially the care standards which has a training section regarding equality and diversity. We also actively seek equality act training. Any discrimination is dealt with quickly and professionally as it is not preferred within our homes. We have regularly opportunities to sit and discuss any issues with the manager. As with most companies we have a whistle blowing policy which allows for any complaint or concern to be brought to attention without fear of retribution.

All staff within the home are responsible for equality, diversity and inclusion, this also has the provision of protection for all service users from abuse and discrimination from each other, families, visitors, staff and services.

The home is currently signed up to the dignity in care charter and staff are all trained yearly in dignity in care by myself as I am a trainer in this area.

Promotion opportunities arise and are forwarded to all homes by email for people to apply. Everyone has the opportunity to apply for job and are all given an interview as long as the job criteria are met. The job then goes to the person most suitable for position regardless of age, gender, race or disability.

A good way to champion diversity and challenge discrimination is to make the care given person centred. Having person centred care means the individual helps choose the care they receive and in what ways we can best support them. We have resident meetings monthly which asks the service users what they would like to do, what choices would they like to see on menus and is there anything they think we need for the home to improve their environment. Staffs also have the opportunity to discuss issues in the staff meeting monthly, or with the senior or manager in supervisions or appraisals. Religious beliefs are also taken into account by asking for time to attend church, in some circumstances staff would take a client that goes church and would be paid for this time.

We would often have to do supervisions on inclusive practices like community based activities or even health appointments. Staff undergo safeguard training which shows how abuse through discrimination can affect us or service users. We also are able to provide different activities and foods due to diverse clients and staff group.

Training is constantly occurring which we review yearly on appraisals with staff, this allows for staff to be up to date and relevant with new procedures. We undergo AAA assessments yearly this allows for discussion and reflection by staff and senior team on staffs strengths and weaknesses. The AAA along with appraisals also demonstrates the staff wishes and opportunities and what are possible barriers or threats to things occurring.

3 Understand how to develop systems and processes that promote diversity, equality and inclusion.

We have regular tools we use to monitor the effectiveness of the care given. Every year we send out questionnaires to families and care teams, this allows us to have yearly feedback of our performance which becomes measurably because we have previous years questionnaires to compare with. Each questionnaire asks how we are doing in different areas within the home and allows for and comments, concerns or compliments to be made.

Within the home we have the care home guide questionnaire these can be taken by anybody, filled in and sent off to the agency. The care home in turn will receive feedback from the agency on any forms they receive.

Resident meetings and staff meetings encourage involvement and feedback from both groups. These can show effectiveness of service and a framework in which to improve by assessing what the clients want and require and how they believe the home is run, staff also have their opinions and voice concerns within the meeting which can in reflection allow for great improvement.

Every month the senior team undertake the monthly audits, this process of auditing shows what needs to be improved and what has improved. We have several audits one of which is comments, complaints and compliments this is where every month we will reflect back on any complaints, comments or compliments received. Our complaints procedure can be found in each unit and residents notice board. The complaints may vary and depends on what the complaint is to what is done with it. Someone complaining they don't like peas on their dinner will result in no peas being put on dinner, which the client can see an immediate outcome to their complaint. An accusation of client being horrible to another client will result in a mini investigation which may elaborate more of what's occurred, usually the outcome is a conversation about treating everybody with respect, and both parties see a response. Something more severe will trigger the complaints book and possible police or safeguarding involvement. This again due to varying severity could take longer for responses to be forthcoming to the complainant. Having resources like the person centred plans and health action plans can possible promote the care given and allows regular reviews by staff and clients. This encourages and reinforces positive outcomes in inclusion. Unfortunately there seems to be a growing concern within healthcare of institutional discrimination this is not always deemed as being known discrimination, its indifference, usually margining groups of individuals due to conditions, it would be like saying an alcoholic doesn't deserve a new liver because they would misuse it. In my sector of care mental health and learning disability people are categorised and subsequently discriminated against due to the idea that they don't understand what is happening. Which is where the mental capacity act should be used; individuals are deemed to have capacity, until assessed to have none.

3.2

When evaluating the tools we use I have to become critical because within the sector I work in families, friends, care teams and even the service users themselves seem to be indifferent about discussing the care. The questionnaires sent to families and teams are sent to everybody which is best practice but we receive only about 2% return on these. The returned questionnaires are not always helpful either as some people that return them have never visited the home or never have contact with their own family. We will always get the regular returns from devoted family members that appreciate the care given and the staff knowledge and involvement. Overall this tool cannot give a fair accurate presentation of the quality service provided. Alongside these the care home forms in the lobby are overlooked even though is where anybody comes and signs in, these are in a basic format and has free posting, unfortunately I believe we live within an age of laziness and if things require even a moderate amount of effort people will not do.

The meetings held by the home for the residents are laid out simply and residents are asked to join, which is not always taken up on. Partially due to their mental health and partly down to disinterest the outcomes of the meetings take a similar pattern, some activities (which are repeated over and over) food choices that we always have and requests for items we currently have and use daily with the clients. The staff try and encourage new ideas and prompt residents to say something they may have asked about a week earlier, now however they don't want to talk. The meetings are generally a great idea but are not utilised to the potential by the service users. The staff meetings on the other hand is a great way for management to discuss home issues addressed to the whole staff group, allowing for response from staff. Training and 60 sec supervisions can sometimes be held within meetings.

Audits that are completed every month again are a real good tool for keeping on top of everything and generate feedback in what area is audited. This process also makes you reflect more as you would have to search care plans and previous audits for the answers to weather things are completed and satisfied.

Person centred planning is the greatest tool that everyone describes, yes the theory is brilliant the service user deciding the care they want and how it's received. In practice it's not so realistic some clients need more help then they think, some don't think they have problems at all. Clients vary in intellect, ability, attitude, capacity and life skills, as managers it's our responsibility to gather the information from previous care centres, hospitals and build up the basic care plans and generate a needs based care plan (see appendix) this is completed in conjunction with service users beliefs, wishes, requests and thoughts but gives a more informative sense of needs and requirements for best practice care. The good is when people contribute towards care plans and express wishes even with family input, there are those that unfortunately won't or can't contribute as well in these cases the client is put at the centre of decision but ultimately is made on their behalf through best interest.

3.3

Improving the current steps we have in place is hard, looking at the questionnaires handed out yearly, we don't discriminate we send to everybody yes the response isn't great in numbers but feedback is good. The only improvement I could suggest is contacting each person personally on the phone and asking prior to sending if they would mind completing the survey. This could improve quantity through greater awareness.

The care questionnaires could be greatly pushed by the home to ask visitors and families to complete, this might increase numbers but could alienate people at the same time, putting a poster above bringing attention to them might be the middle ground.

Residents meetings are really useful tools but with poor turnout and mediocre feedback how useful are they? To improve the meeting we could possibly have a coffee morning with cake every month get everybody involved, hand out paper and pens have the questions on the wall for everyone to see and while having a relaxing drink and biscuit, residents put comments down and post in box on table, staff at hand to assist those that require it. Finish the meeting with a brief meeting giving the notices and round robin for any questions.

Staff meetings are informative and have training at times all my favourite things, however I'm weird not everyone likes doing training. We already try to incorporate different styles and have elements of fun in the meetings. The only improvement here I suggest is staff get paid the extra time the meetings takes then maybe the willingness to have an opinion may be more forthcoming.

Audits from my experience are completed well the improvement here would be rota based completion through the senior team as when one person seems to complete these all the time they become monotonous and repetitive, this could result in the same information or indeed lack of information being recorded.

4 Be able to manage the risks presented when balancing individual rights and professional duty of care.

While supporting individuals in my work setting there are a few dilemmas that arise when trying to balance individuals rights and the duty of care I have.
Safeguarding is potentially the main dilemma I have, as a trainer, champion and referrer in this area I know the benefits and side effects of this area. Safeguarding is to protect the vulnerable within society against any form of abuse weather intentional or not. Dilemmas arise all the time in care for instance a service user showing affection towards staff weather reciprocated or not can be misconstrued as abuse and the service user may in turn believe something is going on when it's not. We have to record and report everything this protects both staff and residents from any allegations of abuse. A resident may confide in a staff member that something has happened but ask for them to keep it secret. Staff have a job that is to protect and safeguard our residents from abuse, we may have connections with the service user but we have to have a degree of separation we are not friends we are staff. In circumstances when the client makes claim but wants to keep it secret we have to weigh up what's being said to what action is required. If something minor we would inform manager of what's been said and record in care plan but say to resident we will keep secret. Something more serious we would have to inform resident that due to nature and seriousness of allegation we have a duty of care to inform manager and possibly police, we can't keep this to ourselves, this could ruin any relationship we have but the welfare of the service user comes first.
Another dilemma arises when there is conflict between beliefs and values everyone is different and has a different value standpoint and belief system. On occasion they will differ from those I support. This potentially could result in poor care being given if I was not professional. Due to religious beliefs as well the balancing rights against duty of care can be hard, an old catholic man may not want a Indian or Muslim person looking after his care but if the other staff are busy and cannot attend then again we weigh up the request, needing immediate help duty of care comes to force and he will be looked after by whoever is available, if not urgent and can and will wait then we can wait for more preferred staff to help.
In my work setting everybody gets a basic level of support to assist with day to day living requirements but some residents require additional support and the home charge 1:2:1 hours to accommodate the extra time regularly required to meet service user's needs. Now weather they have the extra hours or not if the client requires extra support staff will be there to help this is their duty of care to look after everyone.
Finally our jobs are to look after our clients' needs and wishes. This in most circumstances means working alongside family members to give best support required. In some circumstances though my client's wishes may differ from the family wishes and my job is to support the client even against their family's wishes. This also could result in having an advocate enlisted to aid with client's wishes.

4.2

In essence an informed choice is having all the information in an assessable format good and bad and then making a decision based on that information.

To support someone is to be able to make them make decisions but we help provide resources to make choice. We can't let our personally beliefs or preferences affect the choice making process, just be factual with information and assessable making sure the client understands what is being said. Repeating back the facts that is being choose as well is good because recapping the positives and negatives can be more useful than a wealth of information.

We must make sure when supporting an individual we record everything done, said and shown and if in our eyes it's an unwise decision but the client choose to go ahead sometimes we would get them to sign to say they acknowledge we have informed about the risks.

4.3 & 4.4

Mental capacity can be a fluctuating thing that can affect our decision making. Some people have full capacity and make wise or unwise choices this is their right as long as they can understand the choice, the risks and possible outcomes.

Some people have no capacity and have been assessed as so in these cases we still discuss what's to offer but decisions can be made on their behalf out of best interest. Some people have fluctuating capacity or selective capacity, this means they can make choices about some things but not everything in these cases minor choices may not be to interfering but any big choices might require the need for the service user to have a capacity assessment prior to choice. Mental capacity can change for everyone at any time having a disability, learning, mental or physical doesn't mean you don't have capacity. When ill with the flu or chest infection for example anyone could lose their capacity for what is right and wrong for them and times like this doctors or family members usually try and get the individual to understand but if poorly your capacity could alter and choices may need to be made for you.

If you don't have capacity the ability to understand what is possibly good or bad about a situation may not be seen and no matter the information given the person wouldn't potentially understand it, this is when best interest choice is best put to practice.

Everybody who has capacity has the right to make any choice even unwise ones these circumstances will require staff and service user to sit and manage the risk. Simply demonstrated by a service user wanting to go shops that never had road sense by themselves. We manage this situation by firstly assisting to shops, then walking side by side and promoting road safety strategies, then walking a few paces behind to eventually the client going by themselves. A formal risk assessment reviewed on regular trips out and amended as required. Progress can be seen by all the client gets the independence gradually as risks decrease.

CU2944 Lead and Manage a Team within a Health and Social Care or Children and Young People's Setting

1 Understand the features of effective team performance within a health and social care or children and young people's setting.

Team performance can be effective as long as we follow certain features.
In the beginning of the any team setting we must form a team, this can take some time and can be confusing as roles may not be clear and responsibilities haven't been assigned so information flow could be slow and there may be some conflicts.
What happens next is natural progression people settle in and vie for the positions and responsibilities again however there may be more conflict as people struggle for power and challenge ideas brought to the table. The next step is acceptance where everyone agrees their roles and responsibilities within the team, respect is now achieved and tolerance of others views and ideas are more accepted. Once the ground rules are achieved targets are set using the smart principles, strategy is working and further disagreements seem to be dealt with quicker without too much hassle and confrontation.
Once the basis of the team is effectively running further development will occur, this could be adding extra team members to specifically fill a void or job, their roles will already be decided so as not to upset the team dynamics. Within any good team roles can become interchangeable people learning skills of each other and demonstrating effective performance through assessments.
Teams can change quite often people leave and have new jobs so it is often believed that skills need to transferable to others, replacing with new team members requires a period of adjustment and acceptance often the new comer will not feel as one with the team as those in the positions for longer. This is where the newcomer will have to prove themselves have the mental fortitude to accomplish jobs under a strained situation and develop the skills trained, at times adaptation will occur and new techniques are learned from new team members that benefit everyone.

1.2
When acquiring new staff there usually are some challenges to overcome, people are fearful of change so the current team may not show acceptance and the new staff usually are fearful because it's a new role and they don't know what is going to happen.
We have to overcome these barriers, this will begin at the hiring phase we would be clear at what we would be looking for in the candidates for the role. When coming for an interview job questionnaires and application forms are filled out, a good manager will not have prejudice and will be able to see through the nerves or bravado and will be able to make an initial assessment on the candidate through discussions in the interview. We look for the ability and attitude of the staff, will they be able to accomplish the role and fit in to team dynamics.

Once the candidate has the job they will come and start work on a set date and time they will have a tour of the building and be introduced to everyone. The basics of fire assembly points, emergency protocols and job requirements are given. On the first day we like the staff to get to know the clients through care plans so they understand a little better the clientele we have at the home. Through the first 12 weeks probation period the new staff member will be asked to shadow and assist staff, read the care plans and complete the care certificate training which covers all basic aspects of the care industry. Throughout this period the staff member will be under supervision and scrutiny to establish whether they can complete tasks effectively and become self-sufficient in these areas. There relationships and attitude will also be assessed. We are quite a big company with good policies and procedures we like to invest in the staff so we train the staff group up if we believe any staff requires further development or to be supervised in areas until they can achieve what is required we do this. As a group we give all staff the greatest chance of success that we can but at times some people ever do not have the ability or attitude to work in care and will be dismissed before end of probation period or disciplinary hearings.

1.3

One of the biggest issues that affect any team is the old saying "you are only as strong as your weakest link". Teams can work effectively as long as people are completing their roles effectively and in timely manner, unfortunately things can arise in any person's workload that make effect the team's performance. This is where having a multi trained team helps because if someone becomes overwhelmed or is slacking behind others may be able to assist.

The best teams will be enthusiastic and motivated about what they need to achieve, poor morale or motivation can hamper any team and upset the balance that was currently there. Teams need to work effectively and to time scales using a person centred approached. One person can let the team down and change everyone's attitude to the job sourcing this and trying to rectify the problem is the only answer.

Giving feedback and performance reviews will allow the staff to determine how they are achieving their goals and having regular appraisals and one two one meetings permits the staff to voice opinions and determine progression. In our own lives we like to have compliments to be told we are liked and working well this is no different in the work environment a minute to communicate positively in work relationships can change someone's day and make them more productive and spread the positivity. Teams work best with positivity a thank you goes a long way.

1.4

We can overcome challenges to team performance by:
1. Hiring the right staff for the job.
2. Be open and honest about agendas, requirements, job roles and responsibilities.
3. Have clear policies and procedures.
4. Have structured team dynamic.
5. Feedback regular to staffs performance and attitude.
6. Supervisions
7. Training
8. Being reasonable.
9. Non-judgemental approach.

10. Having approachable time to discuss issues.
11. Positive attitudes.
12. Mixture of staff and skills.

1.5

There are three types of management style these may adapt slightly over time and managers even change from one category to another, some managers will be seen as using one, two or even all three styles in different aspects of the work setting.

Autocratic leadership- this is a style that is enforced similar to a dictatorship. The manager tells someone to do something a particular way and wants it done, there will be no arguments or compromise, and it will be done this way. This style of leadership is inflexible and can result in harm occurring to service users or staff because its trained wrong, it can result in negative attitudes and an environment of fear, also having potential for bad inspection reports from governing bodies. On the other hand some places need the set rules, the official stance and may even thrive in this setting.

Paternalistic leadership- this style is similar to the autocratic style, its more fatherly this is when someone leads a team and does certain things for their own good, sometimes protective other times patronising. This style can have a degree of flexibility as discussions should be able to be had prior to the leaders decision, it can again stifle workforce as they may fear speaking to the leader or find what is being said as being spoken to like a child. The good aspects here is that there is more flexibility, more chances to discuss and on occasion change minds. The team may work better knowing someone strong is leading even if not always agreeing with what has been said.

Democratic leadership- is a style where everyone has an input, voices their opinions and decides together the best course of action to take. This is good because it can show greater flexibility and make people feel valued for their input. Knowing the outcome is something that has been agreed in a way that accommodates the majority. The downside is that a leader may not be visible from the group and ultimately there has to be accountability which usual will come to one person.

The best management style will adopt all three styles using different methods when required. Being autocratic towards policies and procedures, being paternalistic on staffing groups and levels and being democratic on activities for example.

1.6

When we look at trust and accountability in care it suggests that everyone must be accountable for their own actions and outcomes, although on a higher level accountability will go up the scale so managers will be accountable for staff and home. Trust is the concept of belief in someone that they will do things right and not cause harm. Trust will be looked at using different dimensions the character which is looking at peoples motives and intent, what do they want to do? What do they want to gain? Why do they want to do it? Then there's competence so looking at the skills and results achieved. We trust and rely on people who have the skills to do the job and we can see they have achieved good results from doing this, this boosts the confidence and transmits trust and reliability.

We will have good policies and procedures within the home, good staff training and supervisions, have diversity in staff group to meet different needs, have flexibility to adapt to different situations, have team dynamics that work, have care plans that are written well and designed to reflect personally on the individual's needs, risks and wishes. We complete audits and have regular inspections to show compliance and quality.These are some tools we use help maintain the trust from the resident, their family and the teams involved, while at all times adopting the accountability of care and actions from the support worker all the way to managing director of the company.

1.7

Conflict within any team will arise, managing conflicts and addressing the concerns of the teams are essential. When a small dispute gets out of hand it can escalate until someone gets harmed (physically, mentally or emotionally) or the care to the service and people we support may get neglected or become secondary to the conflict itself.

Using some techniques could stop conflict arising in the first place by having an approachable manager and clear policies and procedures. This however is usually not enough so having an open door and asking staff to voice concerns to the senior staff instead of escalating on the floor is really essential within our environment, this should help alleviate negative impact on the service users. We must source what the actual conflict is about and separate the individuals from the issue, so if a staff member is irritating another we can move them to another unit, but without separating the problem we can trust escalation will occur. Managers need to separate and focus on the outcome or interest rather than who is in the conflict so as to not showfavouritism to people through position of power. We must than try to arrange options, see what is feasible and how we can benefit both parties equally. Once the options are given then a choice needs to be made that is agreed by both parties involved, the conflict will hopefully have a beneficial outcome for all and should now be settled. There will be times that the conflict cannot be resolved and the management style will have to become autocratic so that both parties will be told what to do and choice will not be given, disciplinary actions may be sought if conflict continues.

We use different styles and methods in conflict it could be one two one, in small group, in staff group, in disciplinary, in meetings or inevitably could be a telling off straight away.

All methods used will depend on the situation, staff meetings and as a group addresses the situation in numbers and clearly defines the outcomes so everyone is aware. Small groups or on to one keep it to those with the conflict and shouldn't then affect the home, the residents or morale of other staff. Disciplinary proceedings will occur when staff are out of hand and resolution cannot be found so human resources will step in and will follow the company's guidelines to the letter whatever the outcome. Sometimes telling staff to behave and it's not the place to argue is enough.

2 Be able to support a positive culturewithin the team for a health and socialcare or children and young people'sSetting.

2.1

A positive culture is encompassed in my work setting by, we use our policy on equality, diversity and inclusion so that the workforce have different beliefs, different interests and produce different skill sets. We complete training within our setting both mediatory an extras like QCF which is paid for by the company showing an investment in the staff group. We complete supervisions and appraisals which allow for feedback from both staff and senior team. Regular meetings or one to one meetings are undertook which allow a time for feedback from staff. Promotions arise within the company and is usually filled by a member within the company which promotes positive prospectus. We will also have the occasional staff treat for example tea and cake after a particular good moment which thanks staff for their hard work. Staff when started work will shadow staff and have input of what is required in the setting as well as information on best practice to complete tasks and help people.

Having a positive culture is also reflected in our service to the care given to service users. We have a person centred approach to all individuals in the service, we have care plans designed just for them, activities based for individuals as well as group outings. We have an in house safeguard trainer, a whistleblowing policy displayed in each unit, and have dignity in care champions. We have a complaints, compliments and comments book which is audited every month.Every year we send out our assessment questionnaires to all family, teams and service users to get feedback and develop ideas on the outcomes. we have regular monthly meetings where residents have their opinion on what they would like in the home for food, activities and décor for example. Our home also completes quarterly magazines to reflect the last three months social activities and upcoming events and send to family's and teams.

2.2

My role within the team is built on three areas firstly I report to my superior, this is where I gather information from those above me in the company who will develop new policies for our homes, these may be adapted slightly to different homes to suit the clients we have and the staffing group, each manager will deliver the policies in their home in a different manor reflective on the needs and understanding of those being instructed. Being up to date and informative about new proposals and the existing rules allows for a confident running service from those in charge of the company to those in charge of the homes.

Secondly I am managing shifts, training staff completed supervisions and appraisals with my staff group. Having knowledge of the service and those that use my service helps me contribute my knowledge base to the others that I support. Putting into effect all good practice measures and guidelines to promote a quality service. Having people to support also means they support you developing your staff group and delegating responsibilities throughout the team can be positive for staff moral and the service itself. Every person that works for me has unique knowledge personal to them that can help improve the systems and service of our home. Allowing for staff to be more apart in the day to day running of the service alleviates stresses on the management team at the same time as the staff are developing their skills and further knowledge which then shows the benefits for all.

Thirdly the service users I work with are all unique and have different views and opinions both on the care and how it is to be delivered and they have different likes and dislikes which promotes the potential for new systems to be put in place. Relating to the service users is quite a key aspect of the job getting to know them how they speak what they like are all key aspects and shows a person centred approach to our care package.

My experience within care tells me that it takes everybody to be working together to deliver a quality service for those we support their families and the staff group, for without the assistance from each individual sector care needs don't get met staff groups work sloppy and deliver poor service, and ultimately with this poor practice ensues and the home could have its doors shut for good.

2.3

Within the care system there are many different ways to manage teams, we could be led by the manager which means the team are given tasks and instructions and are expected to finish these within a timeframe. A self-managing team is run by the team but tasks will be assigned to individuals to complete. There is also a self-designed team that can modify their working systems strategically to deliver the service. Within my home we use all three systems to a degree the manager will hand out tasks and expect tasks to be completed in timely fashion, in each unit there is a team of two who then may divide their jobs to get satisfactory completion. As any good team we have to look at people's strengths and abilities and use these so at times the strategy changes and the team dynamics will alter to accommodate the issues needing attention.

We have a very good training program which starts from day one of employment with the induction process, this lasts twelve weeks or longer if needed. Training is an ongoing process within our home as new techniques are learnt, new policies are made and the legislation changes. We have good ways of working with agreed practices which all new staff shadow existing staff to learn these skills, mentors and supervisors are at hand always for guidance and help to every employee. Over the period of a year we complete at least six supervisions on various different aspects of the staff working systems whether they be meds or personal hygiene. The home also completes two feedback systems which is an AAA which looks at attendance, ability and attitude getting the staffs opinion then the managers which can show how a person perceives themselves to how they are being perceived by senior team. Then appraisals every year allows for similar process but looks at how the staff member wants to develop and move forward identifyingstrengths and weaknesses with senior team involvement to assess and encourage development.

As within any team setting there is accountability this flows from bottom to top and vice versa with every individual staff member looking after tasks to completion and using recording and handover systems to transfer data.

2.4

Within my setting we encourage staff and residents to be forthcoming with ideas to break the current boundary's to be creative in thinking and personalization. The management team within are home we have set legal requirements to follow and these cannot be changed but having innovative ideas to change how we deliver these legal requirements often come from staff attending training courses, or new staff members that have new ideas and a clean prospective looking at things with fresh eyes.

We have an open door policy and staff will often come in with a problem which is when we ask them how they think it should be dealt with, between ideas brought forward by staff and the management team new systems can be developed to manage the issue.

Regular meetings with the staff group also allow for the ideas to flow both from senior team and staff group. We also champion individuals within our homes within areas of expertise or where they have shown potential.

3 Be able to support a shared vision withinthe team for a health and social care orchildren and young people's setting.

3.1
Influencing teams within the health and social care setting to obtain a vision a direction of the care industry relies on a lot of factors,
What service targets do we want to meet? At our setting we want high standards of care and good environment for all who reside and work in this setting. We need to commit to all legal requirements set out by the government and other agencies and strife for a better service by developing newer better systems to ensure clients have a happy healthy person centred life in our homes. We welcome and support inspections and outcomes from partners like CQC and social services, we work with local borough and have received the dignity in care award, which helps promote and highlight how we achieve and could improve systems to give a dignified service.
We look at the level of service we provide being critical and self-reflectiveon our service we ask ourselves is it good practice and what we could no better to improve the service we give, looking into new initiatives and utilising all resources that we have to hand to help us.
We will ask our service users what we do well and what we need to stop doing to help improve the setting and level of care received. We constantly look at the staff team and training and supervisions done, looking into new trainings, developing the staff trying to keep everything fresh and relevant, this should help stop the monotony of "we have done this before" by looking with fresh eyes new styles, new techniques and promote motivation in our group. We need to identify the key areas within our home and the quality we put into them and preserve this with any new staff we have coming and going in the setting.
There are factors within our control for example our policies and procedures, the training and development of staff, then there are factors we can't control for example new legislations, clients family. Then factors we can influence like our resident group by setting good examples for them to follow, providing good care, but ultimately they are independent people with their own agendas we can only help, encourage and impact positively in their lives unfortunately there are times we cannot do anymore and our service can't meet their needs, this is where with team involvement another placement more suitable to their needs will be looked at.

3.2
Communicating our vision throughout the team can be harder than you think. We have regular monthly meeting in which we ask all team members to attend, we do this on a split shift day so we can capture as many staff as possible. This is good because it allows for better information flow, information to be passed on and ideas to be expressed. Unfortunately it has the weak point of night staff not attending because they worked the night before or as always those staff that are not on duty that believe they don't need to attend. We do make minutes for all staff to read and sign regarding the meeting, this again is good practice and evidences the information we have explained. This however has its downfalls again as some staff will just sign without reading. We say if you have signed you have agreed to what has been said

and it is a legal document so if you don't adhere to what has been said then we will seek disciplinary.

We have weekly handover of teams on a Friday split shift this again allows for better information flow. Every time the shifts swap the seniors complete a handover by phone to communicate what has occurred throughout them days so the senior can inform their team, this goes alongside a senior team handover book with more sensitive details in.

The teams have handover books in each unit to pass on what has occurred over the last few shifts and we also complete handovers verbally to night? Day staff as they come on shift change over.

These systems work well as long as people use those correctly identifying needs and occurrences from last few days.

3.3

Working as a team within our homes is only factor to look at when supporting individuals, we must also work as a bigger team with outside agencies and service users personal support network. Using services such as library's and daycentres helps our clients access community activities, we however understand that our clients need support some of these services will support our clients and we must establish communication routes via face to face, email or phone to communicate and collectively provide information to benefit those we support without breaking the data protection act.

Clients teams, social workers, cpns, consultants and family members make up a significant proportion of the clients care team, we have to work together by actively communicating about the individual throughout times of distress, needs and wishes as well as regular team meetings which help establish best ways on how to support the individual in the long term. The responsibility of the individual's day to day care needs fall upon the home as main carers so we must ensure communication lines are open and that we transmit all details to the teams to promote client welfare. Other agencies also play a vital role within the care setting such as social services compliance, CQC and police teams, we have a responsibility to ensure we are open, honest and compliant with these sectors, building good relationships and strong communication styles through informative means allows for a care standard to be met and the clients welfare being focused upon as priority.

3.4

To establish that we are performing well and providing a good care standard we have to reflect and evaluate upon our practices, being realistic and having set achievable targets to obtain allows us to evaluate on what we have achieved and still need to accomplish. Having regular meetings, staff appraisals, monthly audits and care plan evaluations help us achieve this. Having meetings with other teams or agencies will allow for an outside agency to reflect with us on how things have been achieved and new further targets to be put into place to be able to be met on next visit, this gives a timeframe and outcome that can be measured therefore can be evaluated upon.

4 Be able to develop a plan with teammembers to meet agreed objectives for ahealth and social care or children andyoung people's setting.

4.1
Team objectives are common goals, frameworks to work by to ensure clients health and wellbeing. Frameworks are put into place by agencies such as CQC and government agencies such as department of health to meet legal frameworks and legislation. These guidelines will ask for person centred support and being responsive to client's needs, also providing appropriate help and support through timely packages regardless of health and social care boundaries.
To move forward to accomplish these objectives we must ensure that personal budgets are met and staff are trained in the area to deliver the support required, making sure staff have the ability to carry out job and the resources to be effective to deliver results.

4.2
A team consists of varying ranges of expertise from those that are a complete novice in the health and social care sector to those that are specifically trained as a practictionor in an area. Having a blend of these is a good way to build strong teams and keep development of teams for many years to come. Knowledge and skills can be transferable, we learn from each other and have mentors to pass on information to train the workforce of tomorrow. Everyone can be different in a workforce have different interests this allows for a blend of personalities and styles which ultimately benefits those we look after by having this mix.
Although having a good mixed workforce is desirable when it works but at times it doesn't peoples beliefs, interests or expertise could see a bigger barrier than we would like and causes conflicts or negativity with staff not learning and residents suffering.
Reflective practice is a good way to identify the needs and assess the short falls within the team dynamics, this could mean small alterations need to be made to help balance the care package and achieve targets. Having reflective practices also allows us to plan appropriately for future outcomes.

4.3
Team planning is creating systems that allows organisations to assess and cater for the client's needs. We have regular meetings both as our home team and bigger teams for personal clients, helping identify and produce a care plan package that is unique, relevant and functional for the clients. We endeavour to incorporate all teams within planning the care for client's needs, from clients, family members, social workers, CPNS and consultants as well as the GPs. We train staff to participate and develop in their role to attend these meetings and further by care plan writing actively encouraging participation as it then gives a balanced overview of client's needs.
When planning for clients care we must firstly identify the service that is required, giving reasoning and having the common shared principles, we must then ask what outcome is desired from both the care team and client looking at the key steps to achieve the goals, resources required, finances, people and information to achieve them. To be able to make this effective and allow for reflection and evaluation we

have to accommodate a time frame that is reasonable to achieve and establish who will be leading this planned service.

4.4 & 4.5

Within the health and social care sector it is widely regarded that training is one of the biggest aspects to developing a quality staff group and a better service. We must learn and utilise older heads trained individuals to further develop the younger generation and new sector workers to positively enhance the service. We accomplish this by firstly having a consistent induction format which helps to promote the first key skills within the working environment, then progress to shadowing and mentoring schemes where people learn good practice and the skills to competently achieve the desired quality service. Team members will always benefit from each other as they will learn new skills and techniques to accomplish the task.

Coaching and supervisions through mentoring schemes allows the individuals to gather crucial knowledge of people that have worked in the sector for a long time passing down good ways to work, this unfortunately has a flip side that some people get stuck in their ways and believe that they should never change the way of working and then train others wrong which could result in abuse and safeguarding issues. With health and social care sector being a frontline service things change all the time new ways to work new systems and new laws will always be put into place, having a good qualified core staff group will allow for better service transmission and better trained individuals in various roles. Roles within this sector also change quite rapidly this is where transference of knowledge and expertise is a key principle and allows for the blurring of boundaries with staff already completing tasks either under supervision or by themselves.

Everybody that works in this sector should feel valued for their contribution in the way they perform, everybody is different having different quality's and differences also training needs. We will accommodate as much as possible with employees their roles and responsibilities within the care home. We however have a responsibility to those we support they after all are who we are here for and in some circumstances we can try to accommodate everyone as best as possible but cannot always be achieved. This is the nature of health and social care and we can make some amendments to help staff and residents but can't always accommodate everything, this is where the conflict arises and the questions get asked does the staff stay or go? Can we support the individual? There is no I in team but there is no team without individuals. A team must nurture and build confidence and skills in the individuals.

5 Be able to support individual teammembers to work towards agreedobjectives in a health and social care orchildren and young people's setting.

5.1

Within my work setting we have many ways of setting goals or objectives for both the staff group and the home both on an individual basis and more service wide.

Every year we complete AAA assessments this stands for attendance, attitude and ability. Staff are asked to complete their own personal view using a traffic light system and explanation below, followed by a few questions about any training or needs to complete job, looking forward on goals and aims both in short term and longer term periods. These then get assessed by senior team who use their own observations and documentation to decide on colour coding, looking at absence and lateness. Training completed in percentage for ability and looking at supervisions. Attitude is looking at disciplinarys, the staff's performance with clients and co-workers. The other questions will then reflect in the training for staff and possible responsibilities to engage the staff group to meeting their personal goals.

We complete yearly appraisals again with the staff firstly putting their personal opinions down on a range of questions from, what have you achieved over the last twelve months to what do you want to accomplish in next twelve months. Have you any skills that you would like to use in setting to the actions that can be planned to achieve targets. Staff are then sat down on a pre-arranged slot to discuss these with a member of the senior team, the appraiser will help dig deeper and encourage the appraised to give a more rounded appraisal looking at strengths they perceive and agreed targets for the staff to achieve both in training and personal development in any area.

We complete regular supervisions with staff trying to encourage new skill sets and develop everybody to personal expectations. My company has always tried to promote from within the company so it is a key point to develop those that want to achieve and further themselves.

Training is person centred for each staff member, the basic training elements of things such as coshh, infection control and fire have to be completed every year by all but can be delivered in many ways from a session with tutor, in group setting to an individual session or workbooks. There is other training that staff would like to attend or achieve such as the QCF which will be looked at and provided by the company.

We also have an open door policy for all staff to discuss anything they wish to, whether it be working hours, development or even personal issues. We are mentors we strive for excellence by empowering the staff who in turn empower the service users.
As with all objectives we use the smart principle to ensure objectives are met.

5.2

Attached are training charts and agreed objectives to be met in the next few months.

Training plan 2016					
Essential training	type of training	barriers to learning	action plan	date to complete by	date completed

Diabetes 3yr				February	
Fire Safety yearly				April	
MCA/ DOLS				March	
W&P Nutrition Pack 3yr				June	
Coshh CPD yearly				March	
Infection Control cpd yearly				April	

Michael Emery - DEVELOPMENT PLAN & RECORD OF TRAINING

DETAILS	renew	DATE COMPLETED	SIGNED	DETAILS	renew	DATE COMPLETED	SIGNED
STANDARDS PAPER OR COMPUTER				**scils workbooks**			
Standard 1 - Role of Health & Social Care Worker		11/11/2010	M Emery	Mental health awreness		04/05/2015	M Emery
Standard 2 - Personal Development		11/11/2010	M Emery				
Standard 3 - Communicate Effectively		11/11/2010	M Emery	**OUT OF HOUSE TRAINING**			
Standard 4 - Equality & Inclusion		11/11/2010	M Emery	Bespoke - Epilepsy Awareness		07/03/2014	M Emery
Standard 5 - Implementing duty of Care		11/11/2010	M Emery	Mental Capacity Act (Social Care Workforce Pack		20/01/2011	M Emery
Standard 6 - Safeguarding in Health & Social Care		11/11/2010	M Emery	LCC Dignity in Care Champion		17/06/2010	M Emery
Standard 7 - Person-Centred Support		11/11/2010	M Emery	Drug Awaremess			
Standard 8 - Health & Safety in Adult Social Care		11/11/2010	M Emery	risk assessment		15/01/2014	M Emery
NVQ				Record keeping		04/03/2013	M Emery
NVQ - Level Two		22/12/2009	M Emery	Learning disabilty awareness and mca dols			
NVQ - Level Three		18/08/2010	M Emery	Nurse Incontinence Training			
qcf level 5				Pressure ulcer ambition		10/03/2014	M Emery
Essential training				HR&E Charnwood Hate Inc Project			
Medication in Social Care Setting	2yr	22/05/2015	M Emery	introduction to learning disabilities			
First Aid Appointed Person	3 yr	04/12/2012	M Emery	biodose		03/02/2015	M Emery
Health and safety level 2		30/04/2015	M Emery	english level 1		29/04/2015	M Emery
Food Hygiene level 2	3 yr	12/06/2015	M Emery	sensory deprivation			
Fire Safety	1 yr	31/01/2014	M Emery	nappi level 1	2 yr	28/04/2010	M Emery
Moving & Handling without hoist	1 yr	Trainer		3 day breakaway/restraint and advanc	3 yr	11/09/2014	M Emery
east riding - Safeguarding Adults (to do meds)	3 yr	Trainer		health action		03/06/2010	M Emery
dignity in care	1 yr	Trainer		the deteriorating resident		17/11/2014	M Emery
Coshh CPD	1 yr	27/03/2015	M Emery	District Nurse (Insulin Training)		01/03/2013	M Emery
Safeguarding	3yr	Trainer		mental health in ld		15/08/2013	M Emery
W&P ASSESSMENTS				autism awareness		15/06/2013	M Emery
Diabetes	3 yr			Communication Awareness			
Infection Control cpd	1 yr	24/04/2015	M Emery	Challenging Behaviour mental health		11/09/2014	M Emery
W&P Nutrition Pack	3 yr			Tissue Viability			
OTHER PACKS				Sheath appliance inco training			
Mental Health Packs	3 yr	12/04/2009	M Emery				

Michael Emery - DEVELOPMENT PLAN & RECORD OF TRAINING

DETAILS	renew	DATE COMPLETED	SIGNED	DETAILS	renew	DATE COMPLETED	SIGNED
OUT OF HOUSE TRAINING				**OTHER**			
Safeguarding adults referrers		01/07/2013	M Emery	computer ldq cis assignment 201		08/08/2009	M Emery
NCFE - Level 2 Safe Handling of Medicines		23/09/2011	M Emery	computer ldq cis assignment 202		08/08/2009	M Emery
NCFE - Level 2 Equality & Diversity		12/10/2011	M Emery	computer ldq cis assignment 203		08/08/2009	M Emery
cqc compliance worshop				computer ldq cis assignment 204		08/08/2009	M Emery
management mca/dols				computer ldq cis assignment 205		08/08/2009	M Emery
dols		31/01/2013	M Emery	computer ldq cis assignment 206		08/08/2009	M Emery
NCFE - Working with People mental Health Issues		11/11/2010	M Emery	computer ldq cis assignment 207		08/08/2009	M Emery
autism cat b		15/10/2013	M Emery	computer ldq cis assignment 208		08/08/2009	M Emery
Safeguarding Adults - alerters		18/03/2011	M Emery	computer ldq cis assignment 209		08/08/2009	M Emery
				computer ldq cis assignment 210		08/08/2009	M Emery
				computer ldq cis assignment summary		08/08/2009	M Emery
TRAINING OTHERS				LDQ your role as a learning disability worker		06/04/2009	M Emery
safeguarding adults train the trainer		26th 27th june 13	M Emery	LDQ protecting people with learning disabilities fro		01/03/2009	M Emery
dignity in care train the trainer		10/09/2013	M Emery	Care Home Link Day (NHS / Leicestershire Partne		01/02/2010	M Emery
Moving And Handling full trainer		22/01/2015	M Emery	Care Home Link Day (NHS / Leicestershire Partne		05/04/2010	M Emery
				Care Home Link Day (NHS / Leicestershire Partne		14/07/2010	M Emery
				Care Home Link Day (NHS / Leicestershire Partne		20/10/2010	M Emery
				Care Home Link Day (NHS / Leicestershire Partne		21/12/2010	M Emery

We also look into career development with having internal job vacancies that promote those ready to take the next step in their careers.
We use the above charts to track training and highlight shortfalls.

5.3

See question 5.1

Mentoring within the workplace is a tried and trusted way of developing the staff group. This does not mean someone in power, a mentor is someone that can develop and be there for the person. We usually start development from the beginning of employment. The shadowing process where an individual will work with competent staff to learn the job and its responsibilities. This is usually completed alongside the care certificate training that usually ends after the 13 week probation period.

Senior staff are always available for any advice or guidance during the entire employment time. Within our sector we strongly believe that the key staff are those on the frontline they have day to day knowledge and interests of our service users, so they are the best mentors to start everyone on the path in care. People develop over time and through our methods of AAA and appraisals we can identify where a staff member wants to improve or gain further knowledge or skills, with these tools new mentors may come in place so as to teach and support in these areas.

5.4

When using a solution focused approach, we deem that the person can complete outcome using their strengths to find solution. It can become a trial and error process finding things that work by going through things that don't adapting until desired result is met. To overcome challenges we have to focus on the desired outcome, use preferred methods of working that have already been developed but adapt to the situation needed. Having clear steps to follow and evaluating the effectiveness of the step should see a successful outcome. We can't succeed at everything first time of doing so we have to learn from previous failures and take the positives into the next attempt. Through mentoring and supervision we can progress and find a solution.

6 Be able to manage team performance ina health and social care or children andyoung people's setting.

6.1

Monitoring performance in my setting allows for us to identify both good and poor service delivery, allowing for measures to be put into place to correct any concerns. These are essential skills in our setting where we look after people's health and wellbeing, being monitored by agencies that could have a positive or negative impact on the homes survival. Agencies like CQC or contracts monitoring have the influence to promote your home through good outcomes which in turn may provide more bed enquiries or increased fees, or negatively could mean loss of service users, staff and home closure.

Evaluating the progress towards objectives is closely examining the output looking at all aspects of what's working and what's not, not just on a person basis but the environment and climate are taken into account. The climate of information sharing for example can be a doubled edged sword, we need information to complete tasks but we must make sure it is relevant, accurate and complete, timely and completed in a style for the team. The other side of the coin is personal data about staff or residents doesn't remain so confidential and this will cause conflicts.

We have our systems in place to both monitor and evaluate, through supervisions on any task within the home from personal care to care planning. Regular meetings to discuss agendas and prospective targets to meet. Appraisals and open office for discussions and performance reviews.

Care plans are completed with clients to set out joint goals and are reviewed on agreed times to see progress or completion. Training is given to staff through many formats and is required back in timely manner, with help given by trainer. The training will be marked and discussed so feedback can be obtained from all involved. We also undertake monthly audits in key areas of the home highlighting who will be responsible to amend issues and by when.

6.2

Giving feedback to the team can again come in all the same systems, appraisals, supervisions, meetings, audits, training. It can come from formal discussions with senior team and professionals to more informal mentors, family, other carers or service users.

Feedback can be both positive and negative, praising someone for completing jobs well will boost confidence and morale making that person more accepting to develop further. Negative feedback can come in many forms there are unfortunately the times where someone needs telling off for poor performance. The believe that negative feedback is bad is not true it can be positive highlighting some mistakes as long as the person giving feedback can quantify the reasoning and give a better outcome for the person then to me there is always a positive.

The way feedback is given can change the perspective of the feedback sometimes we have meetings where a discussion is held about general concerns and poor performance, this can be misconstrued by some that perform well believing they have done wrong. In most circumstances we have to address the team so we can say it's been discussed and there is a document with the discussion on. Other times feedback from some people we hear but isn't passed on to the senior team. Example we had contracts management in spoke to a staff member and was very impressed with them, saying how well they performed and that they believe they should get a senior team job. However contracts management when speaking to senior team just said how well the team was doing. The staff member was elated at first and then felt demoralised when the contracts management said nothing.

6.3

Recognising performance and completed objectives are very important, from a simple thankyou to nights out. Staff and residents need to feel valued whether this be by completing the task and the delight it can bring to know you have accomplished something or helped someone, to a meal together to celebrate the success. Recognising someone is great and can empower them to complete further tasks but can also shine a spotlight on someone that doesn't want the attention. Team recognition can be better celebrating success as a whole encompasses team effort and boosts morale. We would recognise people on different formats on a one to one basis, team meetings, home meetings, supervisions, and letters, in our magazine or even posters to celebrate our success.

6.4

Poor performance is usually easier to identify, in these cases the first port of call is identifying the poor performer and the tasks/s that they are not completing to standard. The next step would be to have a private discussion to ascertain if there was anything troubling the individual and again explain what is required from them. Hopefully the person improves and starts performing tasks to how they should be completed, when they are not then we have to investigate the situation and show what negative impact it has both on the task and the team. We would endeavour at this point to look at supervisions to explain and show what is required on the task, if performance is still poor we have to look at stage one of disciplinary which is a note to file. The staff member will have outcomes on this again saying that they must complete the outcomes. Unfortunately if after these attempts the staff still don't complete tasks then a disciplinary in the form of an interview will task place which could see staff being dismissed.

CU2945 Develop Professional Supervision Practice in Health and Social Care or Children and Young People's Work Settings

1 Understand the purpose ofprofessional supervision in healthand social care or children and young people's work settings.

1.1

The principles of completing supervisions is looking at the guidelines from in home policies or national picture legislation and ensuring the targets are met through valued supervisions. When completing a supervision it's important to look at the task and the relationships between the supervised, supervisor, the homes policies and the clients we look after.
Supervision are an important tool within health and social care because it allows for task management and reflective practice including feedback. Staff are both entitled to and required to high standards to meet the objectives that are set out by government and agencies including home policies. Supervisions need to be looking at the task and what it involves as well as how the task is completed. Supervisions need to be reflective looking back on good points and not so good points allowing for changes to be made for better performance and service. Supervisions should be informative explaining everything about what has occurred and what may be needed, this can make supervisions demanding and complex so supervisors should have training in this field, but also be a role model for the supervised to understand the job

requirements from someone that can give clear definitions and understand the processes.

The purpose of supervision is to train the staff group to complete tasks to a high standard to support those we look after by means of following legal practices, good practice and guidelines. This will both empower the staff and the service users in the care setting.

1.2

A supervision is theoretically a framework put in place to guide the delivery of a task. There are several models to look at within supervision.

1. Where both parties contribute and are responsible jointly for the supervision sessions formatively, normative and restorative.
2. Interventional – where the supervisor controls the process and will be informative, prescriptive and confrontational to achieve results.
   Orthe supervisee will take control and the intervention will be cathartic, catalytic and supportive.
3. Using solution focused practice to look at end goal and positive ways to achieve task rather than problems and barriers.

Davys and Beddoe (2010) (best practice in professional supervision) looks at a triangular model of supervision with core conditions of support in centre, and links between managing service delivery, focusing on persons work, and facilitating development linked by connections of managing the tension.

This model of supervision is very versatile because while always observing the key areas of support we link why we are doing supervising – policies, procedures, protocol to looking at practitioners work reflectively with the clients and then promote learning. This links to third corner about professional development and keeping skills up to date and the staff knowledge current, also maintaining best practice.

1.3

The requirements of legislation, codes of practice and agreed ways of working influence supervisions in many ways.

Firstly we have the organisations policies and procedures to adhere by this will be formed around legal standpoints but may be changed slightly to be more effective with in the workplace. There are expectations from the employer, service users and carers. The employer has targets to achieve set by law in regards to supervisions, they must be formal, be supportive and informative to enable staff to achieve knowledge and competence, be current and up to date within legal frameworks maintaining competence and improving performance. Supervisions are completed to empower staff to accept responsibility for the tasks they carry out safely and consumer driven to protect those requiring support.

Staff are entitled to quality supervisions and continued development throughout the working life. Managers have a responsibility, a duty of care to ensure the supervisions are carried out to a good standard on regular basis as frontline staff are responsible for their actions and should be trained and supervised to carry the job out correctly.

The eleven professional councils standards are what dictates the legal framework employers must follow the legal framework for supervisions to maintain staffs ability and competence to effectively carry out job.it is the responsibility of the employee however to keep their knowledge and skills current and improve their performance throughout their career.

1.4

When research, reviews or inquiries have been taken in health and social care sector the whole sector learns and develops new strategies based on outcomes. These will then be passed down through staff ranks and will become part of professional supervisions. Having the information passed down allows for greater knowledge and better care practices which improve services for those we care for. Usually a process is undertook while conducting research that has a question that is focused on, the researcher would then investigate the information relevant to the question and be critically while evaluating it. Then comes putting the answers from your question into use followed by evaluation and sharing the information so all in the health and social care system can benefit.
Inquiries and critical reviews usually take place when something has already occurred and needs to be looked at to what could be done to improve the situation and stop it happening again in future.

1.5

Having professional supervision in relation to the employer is for protection. When someone has been supervised and deemed competent to complete task the responsibility and accountability will fall on their shoulders.
Supervisees are protected by supervisions because unless it's documented it hasn't happened, so the supervision needs to be thorough and complete highlighting all aspects supervised and discussed. Without supervision the staff should not be completing tasks. The supervision allows for reflection and feedback and the element of training or further development that would be required. So until fully competent and signed off for the task given the supervised should be observed and mentored.
Supervisors are protected because they have guidelines to follow to make sure the person supervised is competent, they will highlight further assistance required and until they deem that the person is fit for the task they shouldn't sign them off.
Individuals are protected through supervisions because tasks in care should only be performed by training individuals, those that are being supervised are being closely monitored and taught the right way of completing task, the supervisor is accountable at this time and if deemed that poor practice or harm is or potentially occur they should stop supervision and continue task themselves in a good qualified way.

2 Understand how the principles ofprofessional supervision can beused to inform performance

management in health and socialcare or children and youngpeople's work

2.1

The performance management cycle is either four or five elements depends which is used Armstrong (2009) or I & DeA (2007). Armstrong's five cycle consists of agreeing objectives that need to be met, measurement of outputs (so what has been done), feedback relating to performance (critical examination of what achieved feedback to the person completing task), positive reinforcement (agreeing what was done well, and ways to improve), dialogue about development (where the person goes from here, more training required, the next step).
I & DeA four stage is simpler. Plan annual agreements (assessing what is the target for the year), Do supervisions throughout the year (carry out the supervisions agreed in plan), Review formal appraisal process (reflection and evaluation on how the supervisions have been completed, the next steps to take, and are they timely and up to date, any new guidance), Revise and adjust standards (are the supervisions current do they need adjusting, has legislation changed, have the client group changed).
Although these are the cycles of performance they can be carried out in different ways, controlling which is about feedback and allowing for positives and criticism to better control future supervisions. Goal orientated which again is looking at the end outcome and how to achieve it in a way that can be measured and managed using objectives to complete task. Social cognitive is about empowering through positivity people's performance of a task if they believe they can complete it.
Whatever system is used and whichever cycle you follow the finished line is the same, a better service to live in, work in and manage completing the aims of the business.

2.2

Professional supervision supports performance because no matter what setting you are in there is one true aim that is the quality service and promotion of independence for those supported in the health and social care sector. The secondary aspects we would look at in supervisions is support and development of staff and protection for all those involved. When staff are trained from the beginning and supervised correctly through mentoring and management supervisions staff should learn good practice and the legislation to effectively perform and supply quality care. Unfortunately within any health and social care setting there can be cultural differences in relation to other services and this could be detrimental to joint working. The best supervision practice will look at performance and be educational so people can become accountable for their actions and thus in turn will benefit the service. Performance increases when we reflect on the supervisions because it allows for identifying practice issues and those that have good performance in areas and roles and responsibilities may be adapted. With any health and social care setting the staff must contribute towards their personal development and is their responsibility to stay current and informed throughout working life, supervisions can highlight and help train in the areas that there is identified needs to be addressed.

2.3

Performance indicators are a measuring tool to see how people are performing against set requirements. We use AAA and appraisals as key elements to our feedback for performance. We can reflect back on previous appraisals to ascertain if objectives were met and future objectives. The AAA lets us look at performance through ability, attendance and attitude. These can be firstly judged by the person themselves which is reflective then the senior team who will be more analytic and critical. The senior team would have a perspective not seen by a person themselves as the senior team will hear and see things from other staff and service users as well as families and professionals. To have performance indicators we must have something to judge against which is controlled and comparable. We also have to remember that we have to move forward and improve so it's not best to have too many indicators to measure against.

Performance indicators will be factual and not made up from hearsay they are not tools to find faults but tools to improve practice and service. Within any system that is critical however faults will be found but can also become measurable to the extent that is it one failure or many, this could help identify training gaps.

Not all performance indicators can be measurable for example someone that is anti-bulling can't be measured but can be said that they are good at.

3   Be able to undertake the preparation for professional supervision with supervisees in health and social care or children and young people's work settings.

3.1

Within the health and social care sector when completing supervision practices there can often be power imbalances they are inevitable.

1. Supervisions are put into place to meet needs and produce skills to accommodate recommendations from good practice, investigations, research and reviews. These will often be from agencies such as CQC and government. These type of organisations review care standards and will give recommendations to what care should be and how to achieve it. Due to influence of these organisations that could determine whether your service is good or not it is very bias and we have to follow the guidelines they want.

2. Senior team completing supervisions, they are the usual people to complete supervisions but can have power imbalance in two ways. The supervisor can become dictating in style of supervision and not allow for subtle differences due to cultures and beliefs believing there is only one way to complete certain tasks. The other reason is the senior team may not be a mentor and know the staff or client's personal likes and dislikes and again would be rigid in ways of completing supervisions.

3. supervisions can be completed by a mentor or someone skilled in the area within my sector that doesn't always mean someone in authority, in some circumstances

staff can supervise senior team and this itself may present problems to the fact power is with senior team but the supervisor has to assert authority in this matter and may be reluctant.

3.2

Within the supervision process power will inevitable play a major role and should be used to the benefit of all. The success of the supervisory process will depend on the relationships throughout supervisions, there must be a clear defined goal and ways to reach goal. Having and open and honest approach from both parties. The onus to complete supervisions correctly is on the supervisor so they must use the power of supervision wisely. The outcome of the supervision is to gain knowledge learn new skills and stay current with the legislation, if the supervisee is not gaining this then supervisions will be repeated with the outcomes from last supervision used to improve the new supervision.

3.3

Supervisions have certain attributes that should be met during the process that the supervisor and supervisee must agree and work towards when completed the supervision.
Supervisions need to be person centred focusing on the supervisee and their relationships and practice with service users and other carers. Supervisions must have an agreed outcome and target to be achieved using set objectives to reach target. Supervisions need to be focused on the supervisee so must be kept private in two ways the supervisee needs to have space and privacy to learn the task so should be free of interruptions although this is not always easy as a lot of supervisions are focused around the tasks involving service users. The second privacy aspect is data protection, all supervisions must be recorded to show they have been discussed and undertook, these must be kept on a need to know basis and confidential unless judged they need to be shared. With any supervision there are major elements of learning skills and knowledge so the supervisor must make sure there is plenty of information flow to the supervised so they can understand task and what is expected. This of course works both ways the supervisee must make sure that if they need help they ask the onus is on them to make sure they understand what is required.

3.4

Within supervision protocols in our home some supervisions are mandatory and must be completed on regular basis, supervisions such as medication administration these are completed at any time and agreed with the supervisee prior to administering. The supervisions in our home are planned most of the time however at times we have on the spot supervisions due to the need arising. We have agreed targets that every year there should be a rolling system of supervisions and we like eight supervisions completed and on the board at any time throughout year. A general rule we have is every month we revisit the supervision chart and establish who needs supervisions and discuss with the individual which supervision is to be completed next, when we are planning the agreed supervision, how we are going to complete the supervision. These must be agreed by both parties so will become more effective.

3.5

Supervisions can be conducted in many different ways and the supervisor can agree with the supervisee different sources that can be used to achieve the supervision. Supervisions need to be person centred and relevant. We have found a need before that a conversation about a topic will be a supervision because it reflects what has been discussed has and outcome and is relevant to produce better service.
Most supervisions are completed as observations of the supervisee completing a task agreed looking at desired outcome; however observation in practice is not the only method. Evidence can be obtained from several sources, discussions reflecting on practice, team working assessments the workload of supervisee, monitoring the quality of service. Performance measures are used to ascertain the level someone is achieving as long as it is relevant and measurable. Feedback can come from all sources such as service users their families and professionals, all these sources can be used within professional supervision to contribute towards the finished product.

3.6

Completing supervisions require the supervisee to prepare for the supervision as agreed by legal frameworks it is an agreed right of the supervisee. The supervisor and supervisee will agree what is required to prepare for the supervision. There are several means available to prepare by reflecting on previous supervisions and ascertaining any information or questions they will want to raise in supervision or prior to supervision. The supervisee may have their own thoughts and opinions to share so must be ready to discuss these. Preparation is about getting ready, planning the supervision so being open and honest about difficulties or errors previously occurred or current conditions, beliefs or factors that could hinder supervision. With any good supervision there tends to be an outcome to achieve whether it be further training or other actions these can be assessed prior to supervision and carried out if still required.

4 Be able to provide professional supervision in health and social care or children and young people's work settings.

4.1

Supporting supervisees in their practice can be very different due to various areas for example a male Muslim service user may not want a female to contribute towards personal care so in turn would stop the females completing the supervisions in this area. The main aspects to look at for supervisees is level of skills and knowledge, a new staff member will have limited understanding and will require a lot of coaching and information to achieve tasks so would require extra assistance in supervision.

The supervisor needs to show structure and be informative throughout the supervision process and after the supervision be informative and allow for good feedback with the staff member so to move forward and be better prepared in future supervisions.

The more developed staff will also require supervision as laws and requirements change that needs the staff to stay current within their job role. Although established staff may very well know what they are doing they may lack informative aspects throughout supervision. Without discussions and talking through what is happening the supervisor cannot ascertain the staff's knowledge in this area. The role of the supervisor is to encourage the staff to talk through methods of completion. Feedback plays vital roles in both areas new staff and old giving the staff the tools and information to achieve goal.

4.2

Feedback is very important within supervisions it allows for knowledge of good practice and improvements on skills or knowledge missing. Positive feedback is very important it makes the supervisee know they are completing tasks well. Knowing the staffs are valued and their input is valued boosts morale. We have to be careful though because praise should be genuine on things that have been achieved well and shows good practice, but could also be used to show improvement if still not achieving the set goal. Praise needs to be informative and not over the top as staff will not stay motivated and may believe the praise is false, this will in turn have negative impact on the service given.

There are many ways of praising staff from a simple well done orally given to a written letter or poster displaying achievement in areas. Positive feedback for one has a positive effect for all so showing praise to one team member will have a knock on effect and boost morale throughout the team structure which provides an inclusive and positive environment to work in.

4.3

Feedback is an essential part of supervisions and must be constructive so as to improve performance. Constructive feedback will highlight areas that need to be improved and those that are being carried out well. Feedback needs to be person focused and specific for the person on the certain task. The highlight of further development through training or working practices will be obtained when giving feedback. There may be a few areas to improve or none at all either which way using positive feedback and being constructive in supervisions and feedback area will provide a better service and greater trained staff being more effective.

Effective feedback should clearly state what the details are and what improvements need to be made stating why. It must be person centred and specific because everyone is different have different needs and will need different support. Supervisions need to be carried out frequently to keep up to date on personal skills and legal framework. Feedback should show reflection on the supervision the good, the bad and the ugly. This will also provide any measures needed to correct skills or knowledge in supervision. Feedback should be unique to the task supervised not general about the persons working structure because they may be good as general but lack in one area or vice versa.

4.4

Supervisees ultimately are responsible for themselves within the care sector so it is essential for them to participate in there development needs. Throughout the supervision and feedback areas there are differencing opinions. the supervisor will be supervising on legal and organisation framework and will be judging whether they are met or not. Identifying any areas they believe that the staff member will need to improve to be competent and provide a quality service. The supervisee may reflect further on a personal level and identify areas they feel they need to improve upon because they personally may feel the need for further development. The role of a good supervision is to empower both parties to identify improvements; the supervisor must feedback and is supportive for the supervisees needs. The supervisee has responsibility to ensure they have the knowing needed to complete tasks properly.

4.5

Supervisions must be reviewed and revised to meet objectives of the work setting because each organisation will have different policies and then different homes in the same organisation will have different service users and needs so a personalised supervision is required for the setting. Revision of supervisions come from reviewing the last supervision and asking questions such as is it current and adequate for the supervision needed, we then revise to adapt to make sure the supervisions are working for the staff, service users and the organisation.
Supervisees need to make sure they are prepared for the supervision and actively participate in the process with the supervisor. Having a good relationship between the two parties allows for better feedback and should allow for better revision after the supervision.
During the review process the supervisee must reflect on their workload and ask whether they prioritised how they achieved the objectives within a task. The supervisee must understand the requirements from policies and procedures that are in place and the relationship used within the task they are completing. Identifying personal development from supervisions is the key aspect under review knowing what you need to do and why having a measurable timescale to achieve by and be able to revise priorities on development in retrospect to the supervisions taken to better provide a quality service for those we look after.

4.6

Reflection on the objectives of a task may provide details of challenges that have or may arise within the process undertaken. In order to identify challenges staffs have to willingly partake in supervisions and the feedback aspect of the supervision.
The supervisee must be able to understand what has worked well and what requires improvement. The challenges may arise through different areas whether the supervisee, supervisor, environment, task or service user. To feedback effectively and identify needs of improvements we must identify barriers and challenges, we do this by being open and honest in reflection. The supervisee must understand the

effects and consequences involved. Having reflection is not proportioning blame but having the understanding how to overcome obstacles even if that is you, we have to ask have we caused this outcome or how did we influence it. When an obstacle or challenge arises we must talk through it and development better practices to overcome the problems next time whether again through training or other developmental tools.

4.7

Supervisions are covered under the data protection act; they should be recorded straight away being accurate, timely, informative and reflective on practice. Information held can be assessed by the staff member themselves and by those that are required to know information pertinent to the service and to show the staff have the knowledge and expertise to complete task.
The senior team will have permission to know about supervisions so they are aware of the workers standing in the workforce. Some outside agencies such as CQC and contracts monitoring will ask permission of the person prior to looking at personal files.

5 Be able to manage conflict situations during professional supervision in health and social care or children and young people's work settings.

5.1

Health and social care is a unique setting that has a lot of emotion attached to it after all the depiction of what we do is care, the people that tend to work in the setting have a nurturing and carer manor this can throw up turmoil and provide conflict. People may care too much or have different opinions on what justifies good care. Supervisions are a tool used to promote legal obligations and company policies in relation to the setting we work in. Conflict can arise in different ways, some people will verbally shout and air their grievances in that sense, this way to me is probably the easiest way to manage because the conflict is open and can be addressed straight away by the supervisor taking control, calming the situation down and discussing what is required by law and the company and explaining where the supervisee may be going wrong. The supervisee should be able to better accept the response knowing reasoning behind the processes being carried out.
Other conflicts have quieter outcomes where they might not actually filtrate out so can be very hard to manage because the actual reasoning may not be open.
The supervisor should be trained to supervise and observe peoples responses and ways of working this may shed light on to any conflicts as they arise, which again should make it easier to manage.
People's differences and opinions can make a unique quality service however the differences can be too much and the conflicts encroach on the care given to the service users.
When managing conflict in supervision we must look at several aspects these would include being aware of performance or practice issue. The thoughts and emotions

surrounding conflict, knowing what the supervisee intends. With any supervision recording plays a major role where there is conflict we have to be aware of any observed and or reported behaviours so we can produce outcomes to overcome the conflict and provide better service.

Sometimes having a more authorative approach is the better way in supervisions, being instructive and corrective when needed and confronting the problem with feedback throughout process, this may devalue the supervisee and make them feel powerless but will focus the supervision on the problem and not on the person. We do this by informing of behaviour or performance that is causing the problem. We let the supervisee know our feelings on the problem and specifically what we want them to do. The supervisor must ensure that there is a consequence and that it is confirmed to supervisee if they fail to change what they are doing.

Conflict can provide a better service once resolved as long as it is timely, respectful and honest with discussion, we must reflect together and this should hopefully give the opportunity to benefit all in the present and future.

5.2

My work setting has some conflicts that arise within supervision, sometimes it has come about because of a power struggle sometimes due to lack of knowledge, information or insight. The roles taken in supervision must be adhered to and relationships need to be built to work effectively. When any conflict arises its best to handle the conflict quickly and effectively so the conflict is over before it gets to be an issue. I find in my setting because I am a mentor and supervisor that has good skills and knowledge, we discuss issues and pass through them quickly; the relationship we have tends to be more paternal and respectful. There are many ways to work together in supervisions we all want to collaborate and get best outcomes for all involved which is a win win scenario but other supervising styles could end up being controversial and cause confrontation such as competing against each other. When there has been conflict during supervisions I have overseen, my approach is to discuss issues together but stay in the defined roles, and I want to discuss what the problem is and agree with the supervisee what the issue is. We then must identify why the problem arose through our own perspectives and then get a solution an agreed ways we move on from here.

Conflict will not be overcome unless both parties find an agreed solution but the solution must fit within home and legal frameworks. A good supervisor listens but will steer the supervision and possible conflict past the problem as quick as possible before the atmosphere can turn the environment and upset everyone.

6 Be able to evaluate own practice when conducting professional supervision in health and social care or children and young people's work settings.

6.1

Supervisions may be geared towards a supervisor and supervisee perspective but to have a 360 approach to supervisions and to provide quality now and in the future the supervisor must obtain feedback critically on themselves.

While completed a supervision the supervisor must make sure that they follow certain standards these are.

1. The supervision is planned, regular and not changed unless in exceptional circumstances.
2. Both parties should have the agreed agenda that is well structured and encouraging the supervisee to participate to the plan.
3. A private setting to promote positive climate. Have discussion time that is uninterrupted.

The supervisor role is an important responsibility they have to provide information and be responsible to provide the supervisee with tools to complete job.

The supervisor should ascertain with the supervisee their performance and where they could improve in future. We have boxes on our supervisions for feedback from staff group for their opinions on our performance. We then learn and adapt in future supervisions.

6.2

When we receive feedback from supervisions on our own performance supervising people we must be able to adapt and make changes when it is needed. When we reflect ourselves without feedback our own perspective may be of difference to those that we supervise. Feedback is a usual tool for all and will help promote better care and supervisions. When feedback is given we can ascertain a style that has been taken in that supervision practice. Styles such as prescriptive when we had to immediately complete actions during supervision which could result in complaint. Confrontational when we give corrective feedback and whether it produced change. Catalytically which is where we allow the supervisee the opportunity to be self reflective and change their practice.

When feedback is given the supervisor can reflect and can ascertain whether they have been inclusive, impartial and treated everyone fairly, the supervisor's last thing would be to complete action plans and be accurate both in planning and recording.

CU3084 Manage Health and Social Care Practice to Ensure Positive Outcomes for Individuals

1 Understand the theory and principles that underpin outcome based practice.

1.1

Outcome based practice is in basic terms the effect on an individual. This is achieved by contributing care packages that are person centred and delivered uniquely for an individual person dependant on their needs and wishes. The effect on someone's lives and the care received can make a big difference and can aid significantly in rehabilitation.

1.2

Outcome based practice can be very good in theory and when put into practice can be very effective. The government and other agencies compare us against the worlds especially the EU care aspects and there is some concern that we are falling behind due to a growing aging demographic that is more in need of health and social care assistance. Due to the increased demand and the strain on the systems in place it can cause lack of support in the sector. The agencies governing health and social care want better standards and increased care but budgets and finances restrict how much can be achieved. There is always a demand for improvement usually through enquiries and research that change the outcomes required.

Person centred care although is the best practice that is looked for can be limitless and so becomes less effective, there are only so many person centred ways a home or institute can maintain on budgets. We take into account peoples differences and will endeavour to meet needs for that person but at times we have to be more inflexible to create flexibility for example with meals we could not provide a different meal for everyone within a service but having choice of two to three items and then the person making choice of what they want out of the choices makes more choice.

1.3

Legislation can be a major drawback in care but also have positives. The government wants better services for everyone in the sector but cannot provide the financial assistance to make changes needed. The government wants a measurable approach on performance to achieve better outcomes. The framework in care can move at a rapid pace and the restraints and financial burdens on services cannot cope with the influx of care needs. The health and social care sector is a unique service that is funded for by taxpayers. The population is increasing and aging by the extra population increase from the continent and the quality health service increasing life expectancy. The health and social care sector is asked to reform constantly providing more services and better care to match up to private funded countries and agencies in our own country. The outcomes are good and are necessary but are not sustainable. The demand to work longer and do more within the sector puts a strangle hold on growth. Wages for front line carers are not of a high standard but we demand they know everything and do everything to support our loved ones. Financial boundaries in this sector to obtain better staffing and better care will never increase to a level that is deemed suitable. When people get paid less they are less likely to perform to the standards needed. I'm a believer that you get back what you pay into something.

1.4

Outcome based practice promotes positivity and improves individuals lives in many ways, as a professional we look at how it improves individuals self care needs by building confidence. The person centred approach has been measured and shown to have slowed down deterioration of the individuals illnesses providing a better quality of live. The service users often report they feel more valued and respected and so do the professionals that facilitate the care package.

When service users are asked about person centred care they often report they are more satisfied that the processes allowing for broader assessment of their needs, that it gives greater choice and control in the process. Research also suggested that service users had no difficulty identifying a broad range of outcomes they want.

When people are empowered to make positive choices and have freedom and independence to obtain these choices they feel a sense of purpose and self worth. Their care needs are better met and the facilities that are used also gains empowerment by knowledge they are supporting people in a way that is sought after by service users.

2 Be able to lead practice that promotes social, emotional, cultural, spiritual and intellectual well being.

2.1

Well being is described as life going well for someone. Within normal life everybody has ups and downs; ill being is when life is not going well we all experience this in our lifetimes, when we are in grief or sad these are normal emotions although negative. The way we manage the negative feelings especially in care by providing positive outcomes will hopefully promote and influence the feelings of well being.

Psychological well being is a combination of functioning well and feeling good or in other terms physically well and mentally well. To be mentally well we need a range of things in our lives like interests, something that keeps us engaged whether a hobby we undertake daily or once a week. Social networking is a major role in well being having a circle of friends and family however small can make a big difference. Having a job or other daily activity all promotes self esteem and well being.

Having control in your live again however small promotes well being; we all want to choose meals we eat, clothes we wear, time we go to bed and what we do in a day. In social care these small choices make a big difference it is empowering, promotion of input from the outset in arranging the provision of care for individuals is one of the most empowering things a service user in health and social care can do.

Overall wellbeing is a sense of purpose brought upon by positive relationships, choice and independence. Physically well and free from ailments. Support through both the good times and the more emotional times.

2.2

Within are work setting staff are introduced to client well being from the very beginning of employment. The company handbook will have information regarding inclusion, equality and diversity. The job role handed out will instruct staff what is requested of staff during employment. Company policies and procedures are also given so new staff understand what the organisation requires in employment. On the first day new staffs have an induction which will introduce the staff to residents and other staff as well as the home. The initial training program is the care certificate and safeguarding these will give basic advice and guidance on all aspects in care including promotion of positivity.

We have a culture of person centred care within our care plans and staffs are both asked to read and contribute towards them. Each month we complete evaluations with clients on all aspects of their care plans this allows for client interaction and personalisation. The home also has health action plans for learning disability clients which will help enable clients to access services more easily with information about how to communicate, wishes, likes and dislikes.

Staff also undergo regular supervisions under a trained supervisor which will be person centred to individuals when it's surrounding their care package. Personal development is a continuous project throughout the working life both in training in many aspects and supervisions.

2.3

Person centred services and care plans are the basis of well being within our home. The company policies and procedures both support legal and organisation standards that should be met. Having open door policy for service users, families, staff and professionals to discuss issues within the home. We have many activity schedules both as a home for everyone that wants to attend to individual based activities. We support individual's access anything that helps promote well being whether it be to see family, medical services, activities and courses. Each month we have resident meeting and staff meetings to ascertain what clients feel and need, and then discuss with staff what they want how we achieve the and anything as a service we need to amend. Training is an ongoing monthly activity staffs complete from short courses to longer length QCF.

Well being is achievable for those physically well and having networks but harder for people in my service which is mental health, we have to be the frontline and build good positive relationships to build up self esteem and worth. Knowledge of clients their likes and dislikes. Mental health service users can be complex and good plans let us identify support systems to improve standard of living and promote positive well being.

3 Be able to lead practice that promotes individuals' health.

3.1

Within our service we have good networks with a range of medical services, building relationships with your local Doctors, Dentists and pharmacies will help in clients accessing the support they need both at home and the surgery. We also use resources from dieticians and infection control teams to promote better healthy lifestyles and hygiene care. We have menus within the home that have choices of meals for clients to have these are portion controlled and are balanced in dietary requirements.

The doctor's surgeries will keep up to date with client's blood tests which will highlight any nutritional needs and they will issue prescriptions for supplements if needed. Using NHS services and resource tools for training purposes like check for change training. Resources available range from Bristol stool charts to pressure care. Each month we also undertake health checks that will monitor weight, BP, pulse and BMI.

3.2

Needs of service users may require several different methods to actively promote a healthy lifestyle. These would include the social side which would encompass many different aspects from maintaining daily living skills of personal hygiene, cleaning up after themselves and preparing meals. Gaining access to activities from day to day activities of games, cooking, shopping and further education to activities like attending theme parks and holidays. We have to ensure we can promote confidence and engagement for service users both within the home with staff and other service users to community engagement in shops, medical services and further education or daycentres.

Physical activity is a key factor in keeping well it helps prevent disease and stress. Nutritional needs are also a huge factor in promoting health and wellbeing looking after dietary requirements and giving information on disease and obesity. Health services such as doctors and dentist to information regarding stop smoking and drug dependency are aims of the service to promote well being for the service users.

3.3

My service delivers care for those with mental health and or learning disabilities we have many policies and protocols to follow for supportive care of those we support.

Physical interventions can be conducted from ourselves or medical professionals. We would monitor and assist in basic health needs that would include diet and hygiene. The other health aspects we can assist in would be after interventions from services. A doctor would prescribe items such as laxatives and mood stabilisers such as lorazepam and in some circumstances service users would ask for their intervention and at other times we may have to ascertain using care plans and knowledge of clients if they would need assistance. Medical professionals would help intervene in many circumstances within our service but clients will often ask to see doctor, dentist, and nurse when they need to. The staff will assist by booking appointments and accompanying the service users to appointments. The home will book appointments monthly at the surgery for those that have monthly depo's or bloods.

Mental health services will also be assisted to obtain by staff at the home whether its consultants, CPN's, social workers or hospitals. MCA, DOLS and IMCA's are also interventions that can be obtained by staff or professional to assist or restrict service users at times of need.

Our home refers to detailed care plans that offer a lot of information to assist with clients well being while accessing services. Reference to professionals and information resources they can contribute assist in service provision. Family and friends and client history helps build a picture of support needs for individuals and best way to support them.

3.4

Training and supervisions are the tools used to assist staff to provide a unique qualified service for those in the home. Training commences with the care certificate which is the basic foundations for people working in care. We have many training projects to complete in an ongoing development plan that will be up dated regular to keep a quality trained informed staff group keeping up with the demand on the sector. Person centred care packages will differ and evolve throughout client's lifetimes, new legal frameworks and reviews will change and this will need communicating to staff and keep personal development current. Our plan in the home is based on essential learning needs such as equality and diversity, first aid, care planning to name a few. Then home specific training such as MCA/ DOLS. These will be completed along with short courses that assist in looping in policies and procedures and supervisions to give a balanced development plan.

We will use many training organisations such as the NHS and local authority to national qualification courses and in home training to deliver training.

4 Be able to lead inclusive provision that gives individuals' choice and control over the outcomes they want to achieve.

4.1

Individuals have choice and control in decisions influencing their day to day needs and care package support. Talking directly from my services point of view which is mental health this will be arranged and delivered from the beginning when the service user becomes unwell and will first enter the system. Client's mental health would have deteriorated to a degree they were deemed unfit to look after themselves or possible they could cause harm to themselves or others. Most people therefore would have been taken into a hospital setting under the mental health act sectioning procedure. During this initial transfer the person would be admitted to a local hospital facility. While in hospital clients would receive medical treatment and support from services. This part is not particularly person centred as the service user is detained and will be issued a mental health team without much say in the process.

When the client is more medically stable through treatments and therapy it will be looked at for more suitable accommodation for the service user to move to. This transfer process will take place with client preferences in mind. Discussions with their team will enable the team to locate a service in a location of the client's choice. This could inevitably mean moving districts or counties to be closer to support networks of families and friends. When the client decides on a location the social worker will look at homes with vacancies in the area. The client will be informed of homes available and through a process of the home assessing client's needs and client visiting service it will then be agreed this is a suitable place to move client.

The next step is budgets the homes assessment would state the level of support needs the client will need in reference to data provided by the team. The budget will be sent to the funding body that will agree or will want changes made to make more financially viable. When finances are agreed the client will start a system suitable to them to move in this could be an immediate transfer with little support or a gradual transfer that could take years with a high level of support.

Once the client enters a home the homes care package will begin looking at historic behaviours and medical conditions along with clients wishes, beliefs, cultural needs, likes and dislikes to complete an all round unique care package tailor made for that individual.

Whilst in the care home risk assessments may need to be carried out on certain aspects in the clients care needs to ascertain safety. Choice and independence are given in many ranges from meal choices, room decor, key workers and activities to positively give freedom and our joint objectives agreed by all parties to support individual's rights.

4.2

Individuals can achieve positive outcomes when resources are managed well. Within the setting we have to achieve the goals of the home which is to provide a safe living environment promoting independence and inclusion. The service users having choice and rights to do what they want as long as it is legal and safely achieved are a major goal that reflects on the service and the client's lives. Having clear cut defined outcomes of what is agreed and achievable for individuals and working practices needed to achieve individual goals.

Using the care plan, the client's professional team and resources in the community like libraries and colleges alongside in home policies and procedures and the key worker system should allow for many achievable positive outcomes being met for the service users.

4.3

Achievable outcomes must be evaluated and monitored regular for both compliance and effectiveness. We have to look at the resources that are used whether it is finances or suitable staffing levels to balance against activities the client undertakes. The activity level may be high but still may not be beneficial to the service user the whole aim is for the activities to be suitable and promoting self worth for the clients. This measures the positivity and happiness of the client. Monitoring the activities with the available resources lets us know whether they are suitable for the client or will need changing to have the positive impact on the person's life. During the evaluation process it may be deemed that there are too little resources to adequately give a quality service and further investment may need looking into. It may deem the activities undertaken may not be effective enough that changes however little may have a dramatic effect on the individual and increase positive outputs.

4.4

From the outset of employment the staffs undergoes various different training courses which are an ongoing development plan for them to achieve to promote the needs of the service and those looked after within the service. We complete person centred training and we do supervisions to help inform and train the staff group on clients needs and the agreed ways of working according to law and the organisations policies. We have clear outlines of choice and independence for staff to follow to allow for clients to achieve empowerment.

The client group we look after are empowered to make choices even the risky ones as long as we ensure they have an informed choice outlining the risks and possible outcomes. Our home develops clients to access community activities and social development skills also looking at life skills. The staff will work in partnership and even become role models through key working to further develop clients to integrate them as per their wishes and care plan.

4.5

The completion of outcomes needs to be effective, measurable and transparent. This will be achieved through feedback and recorded processes, this can be done in many ways with the main health team on regular yearly meetings and or in house monthly during evaluations. The outcome needs to be defined by the person in their perspective which should be an achievable target. In the initial assessment ideas would have been discussed on how the outcomes can be achieved through the different measures available to use both health and social.

The next step is evaluation and recording outcomes based on the information given and will show to both service users and the team ways to act on the data. This process will also require feedback from the service user to how they believe the service is meeting their needs. With all the information to hand we can re evaluate the care package and even set new targets to achieve and processes to make the targets, or new objectives on current targets to meet the target that may not have been met.

5 Be able to manage effective working partnerships with carers, families and significant others to achieve positive outcomes.

5.1

The idea of a complete and inclusive care package must be that, the care package consists of the professionals, the care team, the individual and their friends and family. Besides the individual the people that generally know the service user best is the family and friends. Information obtained from the family can give a much better care plan because they should no more history than anyone about the person. The service user may not be able to express themselves because of communication issues or anxiety and the family may be able to gather more information and give support to the service user at these times.

Service users will often feel isolated and think that people are against them or not looking after their needs, the family bridges a gap gives support and allows the service user a familiar face to discuss problems with.

At times some families can be overpowering and have ideas for their family member that is not wanted by the service user this is where the staff will support the individual to make their own choices and support them against their family to achieve their own wishes.

5.2

Carers and family are a huge part in service user's life's they are the central nerve that can be the only connection to the community that the service user has. Carers have their own lives and needs both for themselves and those they support their personal needs will often be overlooked because they focus support on the service user. Most carers often neglect themselves and will suffer from ill health, also suffering from poor social networking as the carer becomes isolated.

Support services need to be in place from the social services department, these services could provide financial help and social help. Care homes and daycentres could be located to assist either full time or on a daily basis. Respite is another option to give the carers a break and to allow them moments of normality in their lives.

I work in a care home we actively encourage participation from service user's families to visit, take out, and help facilitate social inclusion either solely on their own basis or with staff support. We have regular parties throughout the year that families join in and enjoy with their loved ones. We complete magazines to keep families aware of what their loved ones are doing. We have an open door policy to allow family to speak to senior team and discuss plans or issues. During the care plan writing phase we speak to family and gather information on how best to support service user and them during the time of admission.

Families will be contacted as per instructions if the service user wants to see them or they become unwell. We take into account family's wishes as some would prefer a lot of contact while some want no contact, our role is to support and facilitate all wishes.

5.3

Conflicts can arise in services between the service, the service user and family. This can be a tricky situation the individual has rights to attend and complete any activity they want to, this is their wishes although at times the family and service may decide it could be unsafe. The factor that arises is the family may believe that the client may get hurt in some way, but this is a choice we have a responsibility to keep the service user safe from harm but we must promote independence. We would seek out information and speak with all parties involved and try to promote positive risk taking with informed choice. The wishes may not be the family's choice but if the client undertakes a mental capacity assessment and is deemed to have capacity then this becomes their choice to make.

Sometimes we have the responsibility of protection from family who want the service user to do something but the client doesn't want to again we have to support the individual in informed choice. We have to respect the family and discuss reasoning and why the outcome they wish won't be met but can ascertain an outcome suitable for all parties.

The service users sometimes will be very inappropriate in choices this can be hard if they have capacity to stop them making the choice, the family and service at this time must try to persuade client not to undergo activity but by means of supported choices, we will give options, give all possible alternatives and information about choices and try to gently persuade them of a more appropriate choice.

5.4

The mental capacity act deems that everyone has the capacity to make their own decisions unless deemed not to through completion of a mental capacity assessment. This within care means that the service users has the right to choose what they want to do and how they want to do it as long as it is legal and informed. This act can put strain on relationships with services and families as the service must upheld the client's choices.

Data protection act ensures safety of client's information; it can only be shared amongst them that have a need to know detail or clients permission to see the information. This again could put strain on the relationships because clients may wish family have no involvement.

Carers and families have rights under the carers act, that says that they must be part of the care initiative for their loved ones but this act can be negated by the client themselves if they have capacity.

5.5

The data protection act is a law which states legal obligations within information sharing and recording. Data must be recorded using proper language, timely, factual unless stated opinion, complete. The information must be stored securely and only shared with those pertinent to the persons care needs, but only the information relevant to the professional in question. The client will have access to their care plan and information whenever they want to and can decide if they want it shared with anyone else.

CU3085 Safeguarding and Protection of Vulnerable Adults

1 Understand the legislation, regulations and policies that underpin the protection of vulnerable adults.

1.1 &1.3

Safeguarding of vulnerable adults (sova) or protection of vulnerable adults (pova).

Adult protection as a whole has taken a back seat of recent years to allow for greater change in child protection services. Abuse itself has become complex due to human rights initiatives in society.

Abuse is a violation of someone's human or civil rights by any other person. This is now more prominent in society with many activist groups lobbying government regarding laws in place. Human rights are there to be beneficial to support everyone in every state of society, the do gooders have in my opinion taken human rights to a whole new level and there are many discrepancies I personally disagree with, for example prisoner human rights they deserve to be treated fairly and with humanity but the victims end up with less rights than those convicted.

Protection of vulnerable adults leans more towards making decisions for someone rather than with them.

Legislative support:

No secrets act (2000) guidance from serious incidents that lead to abuse- this act was derived to ensure compliance with the human rights act.

Safeguarding adults act (2005) this was developed from the no secrets act and separated protection from safeguarding- protection was deemed only for those who lacked capacity.

Mental capacity act (2005) this set the benchmark and set 5 key components to assess capacity, protecting them that was deemed not to have capacity.

Deprivation of liberty safeguards (2008) built upon the MCA and looked at ways to protect people's human rights when they are unable to consent through means of mental impairment.

Law commissioner review (2011) this review was a real trend breaker changing terminology used from a derogatory (vulnerable adult) to a more acceptable (adult at risk).

Safeguarding of vulnerable adults or more commonly known as simply safeguarding highlights that people have the right to take risks as long as they have capacity and informed choice. The best way to safeguard an adult is to let them safeguard themselves.

Legislative support:

Human rights act (1998) (2000 UK) this act states how people have the right to live free from abuse and persecution, violence or torture. Having the right to choice and independence. This act allows services to establish whether they uphold people's rights by setting a controlled benchmark.

Care standards act (2000) this was a unique act that led to national minimum standards of care and a way to measure care standards.

Valuing people (2001) this legislation is supportive for people with learning disabilities with civil right values of choice, independence and inclusion this was the paper that started a personalised approach in care.

Safeguarding adults (2005) although it is used to protect the people without capacity it was the act that emerged safeguarding as we know it putting emphasis on informed choice and risk management, letting service users make choice rather than the authorities taking control.

The fraud act (2006) and the safeguarding vulnerable groups (2006) have roots that were started in the MCA but didn't have enough detail, these acts were to safeguard people from abuse of the fraud offence, misuse of monies and legal powers such as power of attorney.

The health and social care act (2008) and subsequent amendments established CQC who were to regulate services using essential standards and 28 regulations which had a shift towards outcomes.

Law commissioner review (2011) this review was a real trend breaker changing terminology used from a derogatory (vulnerable adult) to a more acceptable (adult at risk).

Statement of government principles on adult safeguarding (2011) this set out six key principles that care communities should support and encourage these are: empowerment, protection, prevention, proportionality, partnership and accountability.

In conclusion protection of vulnerable adults is an out dated concept that mothers people rather than supporting them in choice and independence. Safeguarding is a fresher more in-depth concept that encompasses all the good aspects of protection but empowers individuals to choice rather than dictating the care they receive.

1.2

Since the new policy changes in safeguarding occurred our service has seen quite a few changes from the simple forms at the beginning of employment (dbs) to training requirements.

The client's health and social well being are now more prominent with more emphasis put on person centred values such as choice, independence and client input. The systems have changed from the culture of protecting someone from harm regardless of the client's opinion to support to make decisions.

Clients are assisted and supported to make choices have control funding became more available to meet social needs instead of just health needs, the whole ethos has changed from management of illnesses to prevention and interventions. These were laid out in several white papers culminating in the edition mentioning the four areas addressed. (Putting people first 2008).

Safeguarding started taking on an approach that co-operated services making multi-agency teams rather than individual team members working separate with different goals and objectives focusing on their service outcomes not what is best overall for the client. Funding and further services then become easier to utilise. Safeguarding adults reviewed the no secrets document and believed change needed to occur to make service users be empowered to maintain their own safety. The report (department of health 2009) said "safety at the expense of other qualities of life, such as self determination and the right to family life" the report said there needs to be balance between safeguarding and independence. This is where the services are now asking clients their wishes and giving support through informed choice to achieve goals.

We now have a governing body CQC that investigates and monitors health services, this assists both in training and the quality of services unified throughout health and social care.

In Leicestershire the county has a safeguarding adult's board that any issues surrounding a clients safeguarding can be discussed and investigated. Emphasis on CQC outcomes, governmental reviews and MCA/ DOLS changes are still being modified and are more prominent.

1.4

Serious case reviews and inquiries have changed the views and opinions on adult social care by the public. There is a higher emphasis on quality care due to a more aging population and the requirement for more services to be available. The government has not increased funding enough to meet the increase in this service over the recent decades and the monitoring of the service provision was not as scrutinised as should have been.

CQC was born out of a necessity for clarity to monitor and inform services and to regulate the care industry in its entirety. The managers in care now need to be more proactive to guard against failings and abuse. The BBC panorama program have been at the heart of inquiries by going undercover and highlighting failures in care such as winterbourne view where the level of abuse called for a serious case review by the government and resulted in changes in care being achieved.

Throughout all reviews and inquiries there was an emerging theme that was the lack of management skills and transparency, poor inductions, training and supervisions that let poor practice carry on unchallenged. CQC have developed training put into place for inductions in the homes which is now known as the care certificate. There is greater emphasis on staffs abilities and training when the homes get inspected. The homes can be assessed at any time and must be open and honest showing transparency of all aspects within the home during inspections.

1.5

Protocols to follow in my organisation if suspected abuse or harm has occurred are as follows.

Client or staff member alert to possible abuse occurring.

Client is made safe or harm, abuse stopped (in case is occurring now) (preserve evidence)

Manager/ senior is informed (trained referrers)

Assessment of situation (injuries, what occurred)

Services like police/hospital/doctor are utilised if required at this point.

Incident reports/ accident books to be completed.

Investigation will be made by police if need be or home to ascertain abuse. (Lead will be held with most appropriate system, no not ask leading questions)

Client teams will be informed.

Riddor/ health and safety inspectorate/ CQC / safeguarding services at local council informed.

The notifications will happen to services quickly and may be in different order some will not be included it all depends on the incident and seriousness. There may be issues surrounding capacity and consent this may require MCA.

2 Be able to lead service provision that protects vulnerable adults.

2.1

Within the health and social care sector the guided principle of keeping people safe is still adopted, this is not the preferred method now. The belief that people should take responsibility for their own safety has been made and that we the carers should support the individual. Clients should be able to make risky or unwise decisions as long as they have capacity and informed choice. The empowerment to service users through person centred approaches promotes choice, privacy, rights, dignity, respect and independence this should help eliminate abuse as the person is in charge of their lives.

There are different ways for us to empower people.

Firstly the client may have no road sense for example so is deemed a hazard for the client to walk to local shop by himself. The home would complete a risk assessment with the client that is personal to him highlighting the hazards and outcomes. From the initial risk assessment a plan would be made to empower client. We would walk with client to the shop and teach the client road sense at the same time, this would be done by using safest methods appropriate such as staff walk curb side, use traffic lights and crossings. This system of escorting may be required for several trips and the aim would be to cut down on assistance by following a few steps behind, then further behind, to the final outcome of client goes by himself and staff monitor through time and appearance. The risk should decrease and the assessment can change to reflect this at every stage until independence is found.

Secondly the client may wish to skydive all the team believe this is a risky task to undertake but the home has a culture of empowerment. The client will be asked who they would like to go on the dive with. The person involved will then gather evidence on the skydive looking into every possibility form location, price, dates, types of skydive. They would also look at the positive outcomes and possible consequences to the dive. This information will be shared with the client in a balanced and informative way. A risk assessment would still be carried out. With information, consequences and risk assessment the dive can be carried out to the safest possible way, this does not eliminate risk but gives positive risk taking.

2.2

When speaking to staff about abuse we would discuss the types of abuse.

Physical- may have bruises, scratches, marks – caused by hitting, kicking, scratching.

Sexual – may have bleeding, bruising, isolation – caused by rape, inappropriate touch, pornography without consent.

Psychological/ emotional – isolation, self harm, loss of appetite – name calling, taunts.

Institutional – isolation, malnutrition, no dignity – strict bedtimes, no choice, understaffed.

Self neglect/ neglect – unkempt appearance, smelly, sores – leaving people in bed, refusal to shower, not turning clients.

Financial – no money, no belongings, begging – misuse of power attorney, stealing.

These are but a few types of abuse, signs and symptoms the lists can be endless and would be fully trained by myself as I am a train the trainer in safeguarding. The main aspects would be bruising and change in behaviour, but we have to be careful because only because someone has a bruise doesn't mean abuse has taken place, our roles and responsibilities is to report and record.

Measures to stop abuse occurring will consist of good care plans, person centred approach, choice of meals, open door policy, whistleblowing policy, staff training and supervisions, the home keeping up to date with new legislations, keyworkers, and family involvement.

Steps to take if suspected abuse has taken place will be to make client safe, report incident, fill out paperwork, be supportive, do not make promises, do not tell alleged perpetrator, do not investigate yourself, no not ignore. The alerter role is to alert and support not refer and investigate.

2.3

To identify systems in place at my work setting we have to break them down to categories policies and procedures.

Policies ; whistleblowing policy, safeguarding policy, recruitment policy, finance policy, discrimination policy, equality, diversion and inclusion policy, medication policy, personal hygiene assistance policy, food and drink policies, training policies, supervision policy, relationship policy, data protection policy, health and safety policy.

Procedures; risk assessments, training, supervisions, person centred care planning, open door, complaints, recruitment.

There are many policies and procedures in place within the workplace that I haven't mentioned but all policy and procedures are in place to minimise risks and chances of abuse occurring.

2.4 & 2.5

To monitor the effectiveness of policies and procedures we use many tools:

Meetings (staff and resident) this gives provision for feedback on any issues that need discussing, any training that needs to be achieved, client happiness and staffs happiness. The meetings will also have the advantage of general discussions that will then be recorded so must be acted upon.

Audits will be undertaken monthly on many aspects like medication, falls, care plans, infection control, complaints comments compliments, safeguarding, cleanliness. These audits will be completed by senior staff and feedback to the team during meetings and training, supervisions so they are aware of good practice and poor standards, these can then be addressed and rectified.

Spot checks will be carried out on some occasions throughout every week to ensure the clients are getting what is paid for and staffs are complying with the policies and procedures.

Supervisions/ appraisals will take place throughout the year and allow for feedback from superiors and staff to discuss shortfalls and quality standards and ways to improve to meet the standards wanted by the company and other agencies.

All the systems used together create a very informative system that allows for feedback to everyone in a positive and constructive way, with the main aim being service users well being and safeguarding through our policies and procedures.

3 Be able to manage inter-agency, joint or integrated working in order to protect vulnerable adults.

3.1

Partnership working in health and social care cam about from the no secrets (2000) act and was further expanded upon in safeguarding adults (2005). This set out a national framework which stated how partnerships should be formed and operated. Prior to partnership working different sectors worked independently and had a reluctance to share information and resources which in essence slowed all the safeguard processes down and was technically a form of abuse in itself.

Local councils were asked to form safeguard boards as a result and these would have a range of services included to gain the best result for people being safeguarded. The safeguarding board would be made from many agencies including social services, PCT's, housing, education, welfare, CQC, voluntary sector and the independent sector.

There may be many agencies listed here but the expertise will be used in many different cases not every case. We have a major safeguarding occurring currently the team consists of social worker, CPN, consultant, safeguarding, DOLS, IMCA, service user and ourselves.

The main objective is the outcome for the client trying to keep the rights of the individual while keeping them safe. The person is in the centre of the decision at all times but capacity may need to be assessed and continuous could be done in best interest. The issue regarding safeguarding has to be reported from one source then the safeguard team will start investigation. One element of the team tends to take lead in safeguarding this tends to be the main area of concern so could be health or social. Boundaries would have to be discussed, what is the problem, what is the desired outcome, how and why we can achieve. The panel will have different responsibilities to achieve whether it be safeguarding client now, or looking into financial assistance. Information between the team must be free flowing to ensure everyone in this multi- agency force has all the information to make informed decisions. With any safeguarding and team there are limits to what an individual can do, they might need further assistance to move things further for example a CPN is technically a nurse and cant issue prescriptions or change medication this is a consultants job. Decision making has to be agreed by all this process is again safeguarding in itself not one person can decide an outcome without panel decision. As with any process in care, recording is a main process because it allows for written confirmation on what is happening and will be shared to all those in the panel.

3.2

Partnership working has advantages and disadvantages, the improvements over the last few years has made it easier to access safeguarding teams but they have so many referrals the response time can be severely delayed. The teams involved in safeguarding do have client in mind when making decisions but they all have their own opinions on things should work. We are at the deep end looking after the client while the safeguarding is occurring and find the feedback can be slow and inconsistent. There can be differences in opinions that will not be negated so the safeguard ends up being stalled. Teams such as IMCA and DOLS are important teams for the client and us but they tend to have differing views to other services such as health and social so on occasion conflicts arise. The overall project of multi agency working is really good the idea that several teams get involved to protect and safeguard the individual rather than one team that doesn't have experience in all areas, this slows down the process and has the potential to put the client at further chance of harm.

From the care home point of view we would like to see more inclusion, agreements to be quicker accessed because the client is in need but delays often occur either in finance or housing and this puts client in harm's way. The teams to visit more often in the period while at risk. More training for those further up in the decision tree. Client first not money.

When the processes work they are very effective and get the client in a safe living environment in a desired location quickly without too much turmoil.

4 Be able to monitor and evaluate the systems, processes and practice that safeguards vulnerable adults.

4.1

Safeguarding adults is the responsibility of everyone both in the care industry and those not in care. The service users have a responsibility in line with safeguarding adults (2005) to protect themselves. Person centred care and safeguarding was adopted and called for service users to be more involved in both care planning and safeguarding themselves.

Empowering individuals to make informed decisions and have knowledge of what is constituted as abuse is a good idea but is also difficult. Many people in the setting have an illness that may impede on cognitive functioning. This could be dementia, mental illness or learning disability. This does not mean that the rights to be included or have the information both made available and taught are not essential but highlights the possibility of poor understanding and possible misuse.

We support the individuals through residents meetings and on a one to one basis giving information to clients on what constitutes as abuse, how to spot abuse and reporting of abuse. We have complaints procedures forms all around the home so the clients know how to complain. Training is offered to staff on safeguarding and clients are asked if they want to join in any sessions to better get an understanding of safeguarding.

During meetings and one to one clients are asked how they feel they have been treated and how we can support them to obtain better quality and a safer living environment.

4.2 & 4.4

Looking at procedures we have in place within the home to protect at risk adults it can highlight the effectiveness but also have elements of improvements.

Complaints and comments procedure – staff are trained on receiving complaints and comments and the procedure to follow when recording, these will be investigated by senior team and acted upon to resolve complaint and then give feedback to the individual on the response. This will then be audited every month. Each block in my setting has a copy of the complaints procedure so both service users and families know what to do, this will also be talked about in resident meetings so they understand what they can do. This has room for improvement because the clients could be more informed every meeting and asked if there are concerns they want to discuss in private.

Accident and incident reports – staff are trained through the process of mentoring on how to complete these forms. Residents know that incident reports are completed in case of incident, and injury reports are discussed with clients to fill them out. This can be improved by getting the client further involved and have their side of an incident, asking what made them feel the way they did, what could be done to change situation. Currently all incident reports are filled out by staff and in some circumstances witness statements are completed with residents, but it lacks personalisation and input from the client.

Reviews – clients and staff attend reviews when required, some residents will decline the meetings and some love them. The reviews although about the client and discussed with the client can use language that they don't understand and then they might feel incapable.

Risk assessments – there are two kinds of risk assessment and this is a good process because one will focus on the risk and the hazards involved from the home and staffs perspective. The other one is more personalised and allows the input and agreement from clients on how the risk can be managed and give a positive outcome.

Care plans and evaluations – care plans are written with client involvement to give a person centred care package, and evaluations are carried out monthly with clients getting their perspective and then staff's perspective in one form. The failure we have is lack of interest from clients when it comes to involvement in care planning. The information in the basic care plan then seems to be more reflective on staff's ideas of past history and current situation. We then take our time to develop person centred care plans with clients help over a longer period that is more suitable for the clients.

4.3

We all hope for good practice in safeguarding but at times failures occur and when this happens we must challenge it because if we don't the consequences for the service users and service could be severe, as well as making the person observing the abuse take place is just as bad as the one committing the failure.

We have strict policies in place and training to reinforce the policies, the policies are whistleblowing and safeguarding. When complaints are made this must be investigated and recorded regardless of validity of accusation, there are times allegations get made that have no founding but they must be looked into.

Poor practice or abuse may be reported, witnessed or observed through practice. We would have to have the facts about the concern raised, why they breach the codes of practice, look at the qualifications and supervisions currently undertaken to ascertain whether the staff new the procedures, we would also need to ascertain any circumstances that may have contributed towards poor practice.

The result of the investigation will have an outcome these could be: no action required further supervisions, note to file, further training or disciplinaries.

To complete an investigation we must listen to all sides of the story although we have a culture of no blame the management are responsibly for good safe working environment for all involved so any incidents must be addressed.

CU3086 Lead and Manage Group Living for Adults

1 Be able to develop the physical group living environment to promote positive outcomes for individuals.

1.1

A group living environment is designed to meet the specific needs of individuals in situations that are as normal as possible rather than institutional care. Group living can include facilities for adults in residential homes, nursing homes or sheltered / extra care housing. Wolfesberger (1975) identified some negative features of large-scale institutions, individuals were segregated from society often kept in degrading conditions and treated inhumanely. Wolfensberger's formulation of the principle of Normalisation means "Making available to all people with disabilities patterns of life and conditions of everyday living which are as close as possible to the regular circumstances and ways "of life or society" this is the basis of modern day thinking and legislation. Over the year's different theoretical approaches to group living provisions for adults have changed the way in which we offer our care services and living provisions. Person centered planning has had major impacts and affected group living in many ways. The approach to current group living provision has moved a long way forward since the days of the workhouse or asylums. The NHS and Community Care Act 1990 called for a more community based approach to care with the introduction of the person-cantered approach, by supporting the independence and autonomy of the service users. Some service users who require special consideration such as people with learning disabilities can still find the need to live in a group living environment, but these establishments tend to be much smaller than the old hospitals. Eric Erikson developed a theory that divides an individual's life into eight stages that extend from birth to death (unlike many developmental theories that only cover childhood). Erikson (1902-94) this means that when reviewing and updating the need of a service user you would not only look at their physical needs you would also review social and cognitive development. Erikson created the eight stages of developments from birth to death using this he considered basic conflicts of a service user of each stage. This table of development can be used to identify a service user's potential conflicts which are relevant to the particular stage of development that they are at. For example when I support the service users I work with I take a holistic approach, I take into consideration developmental needs along with physical needs. I think the positives of this approach are that you meet service users specific needs whilst taking into account age related conflicts and we are also eliminating the unneeded grouping of service users i.e. Group Living.

Maslow's hierarchy of needs is another important theory when considering group living provisions for adults as this outlines the stages that are required to carry out personalization through person centered planning whether it be through goals, risk assessments, support planning or key working sessions. His theory suggests to us that "individuals needs must first be met at a basic level, and then must be satisfied at each level before moving onto the next" Maslow (1908-70)

John O'Brien's Five Accomplishment had a real impact on the way services for people with learning disabilities have been developed and delivered and indeed changed the thinking of many. Papers such as Valuing People ("New Strategy for Learning Disability for the 21st Century") and The Supporting People programme (2003) very much follow these accomplishments. The Disability Discrimination Act 1995 also had an impact by making all public buildings being made accessible to disabled people. The Equality Act 2010 and the United Nations (UN) Convention on disability rights help to enforce protect and promote the rights of people with a disability.

My organisations ethos has always been that everyone should have the same rights and civil liberties, access to everyday living conditions and circumstances as everyone else, regardless of their disability.

These rights include:
Having a say in how they live their lives, and contribute to the decision making process.

Being given opportunities to develop friendships
Being treated with dignity and respect
Living in a homely environment and having contact with family Be given the opportunity to be educated
Enable the service users to feel valued in society
Current approaches now ensure that service users can have control of their lives and the care that they receive. They are included in the decisions made about their care and are encouraged to communicate their wishes, preferences and needs.

Staff teams need to have good training and leadership to enable services to provide truly individualised care services and the service users must be supported to actively participate in the planning and provision of care that they provide.

As Manager of the care home I must ensure that we use appropriate methods to facilitate effective communication with the service users to ensure they are actively involved at all stages of how the home is managed.

1.2

Safe practice is very important to the promotion of dignity in care. There are a number of legislative measures and regulations to support health and safety at work. These are intended to protect people in work, those using services and the wider public. The Health and Safety Executive (HSE), local authority Trading Standards and the Care Quality Commission (CQC) can all bring prosecutions against care providers who breach health and safety standards The CQC expect all regulated providers to comply with their new Fundamental Standards (which replaced the earlier Essential Standards on 01 April 2015). Eg Essential standards of quality and safety (CQC) 2010 regulation 15 – refers to accommodation that is equipped to assure comfort and privacy and meets the assessed needs of the service user. Also all allegations of abuse will be taken seriously and investigated accordingly, In line with the health and social care act 2008 and policy and adult protection.
National minimum standards were introduced with the Care Standards Act 2000 which gave clear guidelines of how care homes should be managed and what standard of care the service users should receive. The Care Quality Commission is the regulator of health and adult social care services and has powers of enforcement.

The CQC now inspect care homes against the five key questions of enquiry (KLOEs) which came into force in March 2015 and replaced the Essential Standards. KLOEs put the service users at the centre of the inspection system and as the registered manager of a care service; I am carrying out a regulated activity which means I have to manage the care home in line with the five key questions of enquiry to comply with the law.

The Health and Social Care Act 2008 Regulations 2014 which came into force from April 2015 makes clear the duties that people providing and managing services have. Key lines of enquiry include: Is it Safe: - in residential care are people protected from bulling, harassment, avoidable harm and abuse that may breach their human rights.

Are people protected by the prevention and control of infection? Is it Effective: - how do people receive effective care, which is best practice, from staff that has the knowledge and skills they need to carry out their roles and responsibilities? Are people supported to eat and drink enough to maintain a balanced diet? How are people's individual needs met by the adaptation, design and decoration of the service? Is it caring: - how are positive caring relationships developed with people using the service? Is it responsive: - how do people receive personalised care that is responsive to their needs? Is it well-led:- how does the service promote a positive culture that is person- centred, open and empowering?

It is a legal requirement for me to display a certificate of employer's liability insurance and the Health and Safety Law poster. I must ensure that my employees receive adequate and appropriate information, instruction and training to enable them to carry out their work safely. I must also ensure the health and safety of employees and other people on the premises and complete risk assessments.

Employee's must comply with the legislation and ensure that their actions do not adversely affect others. They must take reasonable care for their own safety and that of others and Co-operate with their employer on health and safety matters.

The Human Rights Act 1998 includes the following rights - The Right to life, The right to freedom from torture and inhuman or degrading punishment , The right to freedom from slavery, servitude and forced or compulsory labour, The right to respect for private and family life, home and correspondence, The right to freedom of thought, conscience and religion, The right to freedom of expression, The right to freedom of assembly and association, The right to marry and found a family, The prohibition of discrimination in the enjoyment of convention rights, The right to peaceful enjoyment of possessions and protection of property, The right to access to an education, The right to free elections.

Control of Substances that are Hazardous to Health Regulations 2002 (COSHH) requires me to have a COSHH file.
The file we have lists all the hazardous substances used in home and contain Data sheets for every product, which contain advice on emergency treatment protocols. The storage of medication in the care home is also covered by COSHH the Safeguarding Vulnerable Groups Act 2006, which requires me to obtain a criminal record certificate before any prospective employee works with vulnerable adults. The Mental Capacity Act 2005 which came into force in 2007 which states that every adult has the right to make his or her own decisions and must be assumed to have capacity to do so unless it is proved otherwise.

This means that we cannot assume that our service users cannot make a decision for themselves just because they have a learning disability. We must support them to make their own decisions by giving the information in ways that may help them make their own decisions. If lack of capacity is established, it is still important that I involve the person as far as possible in making decisions. I must ensure that anything done for or on behalf of a person who lacks capacity is done in their best interests and I should consider whether it is possible to follow a less restrictive course of action. Where a person does have capacity they have the right to make decisions those others might regard as unwise.

1.3

Risk assessments help managers and support staff so they feel reassured that they have acted in the best interests of the individual. Safety is only one aspect of life and is not the only goal in life. What good is making someone safe if it merely makes them miserable? (Department of Health 2007)

I have a duty of care for the service users that I support and must ensure the health and safety of my employees and any other people on the premises. Risk assessment and risk management are a crucial part of adult social care and I have to balance the needs of the staff and the wishes of the service users, which can be quite difficult in some cases. I have to be mindful that the service users have the right to make choices and to take risks but I have to consider my duty of care towards them. For example one of my service users enjoys. Watching films on the TV and he has said he would like to visit a cinema. He has no awareness of stranger danger or the dangers posed by passing traffic or crossing the roads and is risked assessed as not being able to access the community without support. To enable him to access the cinema a staff member will need to be on duty to support him and transport him. Both the service users have their own rooms that are decorated in the style of their choice and contain their own personal furniture and possessions.

The bedrooms are in line with the National minimum standards by having usable floor space sufficient to meet individual needs and lifestyles and staffs are always mindful of the service user's right to privacy.

The home itself has none slip flooring in the bathrooms and kitchen, all of which are freely accessible to the service users, although there are risks assessments in place for when there is cooking taking place.

The service users are always consulted when new furnishings are going to be purchased or rooms decorated to ensure that things are how they want them; after all it is their home and only our work place.

1.4

There is a close relationship between the physical environment and the well-being of individuals, and some people with different needs will need design features that are related to their particular requirements. One needs to put themselves in the shoes of the service user and their carers when you think about the building / environment. The work of Judd (1997) explores how an environment is designed to enhance well-being. E.g. does the design of the building compensate for disability, maximize independence, enhance self-esteem, demonstrate care for staff, reinforce personal identity and welcome relatives and the local community?

The physical environment needs to be warm, clean, comfortable and safe to ensure the service users wellbeing and to promote their independence and uphold their rights to human necessities and niceties.

By maintaining a high standard of environment the service users will have a sense of self worth and have a feeling of pride in their home, this will all have a positive effect on their health, happiness and emotional wellbeing. It can also promote their sense of identity, self-image and self-esteem and above all make them happy.

1.5

Justify proposals for providing and maintaining high quality decorations and furnishings for group living it has long been recognized that there is a relationship between the design and quality of the environment and its impact on relationships and social interaction. The avoidance of an institutional look and feel should be the first consideration.

The Essential Standards of Quality and Safety state that the premises must be suitable safe and promote wellbeing.
The new regulatory framework, aims to ensure quality services rather than service users having to live with second best. In applying the standards regulators will seek evidence of a commitment to continuous improvement, quality services, support, accommodation and facilities which assure a good quality of life for the service users.

As a manager I have to ensure that all equipment is safe and meets British Safety Standards to ensure that any hazards are kept to a minimum. I have to ensure that staff are properly trained in the use of equipment and that it is properly maintained and where possible we ensure equipment is as 'homely' as possible to prevent the home looking like a hospital

The furniture and fittings need to be of good functional quality and aesthetically pleasing to fit in with the "home" and to promote the emotional well being of the service users. Living and working in an environment that is decorated and furnished to a high quality promote pride and people will value the home and can get a feeling of self worth. Careful thought is given to details such as textures and colours and how fabric feels. It is also important that all furnishings and decoration are of a high quality because if you buy cheap you get cheap and things won't last long before they need replacing that has a detrimental effect on the homes budget.

By providing and maintaining high quality decorations and furnishings for the care home we promote a sense of wellbeing where the service users feel safe, secure and valued as well as adhering to legislation and making sound financial sense.

1.6

A well-managed group living service will strive to be as inclusive as possible when it comes to making decisions about the physical environment. When making decisions about the physical environment of the home we always involve the service users as far as possible, although it is very difficult to fully engage them in every decision because of their mental health and or learning difficulties.

The service users are provided with as much information as possible about any proposed changes and they are given choices.
When making decisions that the service users find difficult to be involved with I consider their past choices and desires, Staff input is also sought to endeavor to make the choices that will be what the service users want.

After all the care home is their home and they are the ones that are affected by any changes, be they large or small.

2 Be able to lead the planning, implementation and review of daily living activities.

2.1

legislative and regulatory demands on group living services are intended to ensure that the provision of daily living activities takes place in an environment where the needs of the service user is paramount.
Legislation starts with the NHS and Community Care Act 1990 which basically obliges local authorities to carry out an assessment of anyone that is unable to look after themselves.
Daily living activities are the fundamental things that people should be able to do in their everyday lives to enable them to maintain their independence.

Basic skills would include Eating, bathing, dressing, toileting, walking and maintaining their continence.
More complex skills include managing finances, using transportation such as driving or using public transport, shopping, preparing meals, using the telephone and other communication devices, doing housework, managing their medication.

When the "needs of Care assessment" is completed the local authority has the duty to provide services to meet the identified needs.
The Health and Social Care Act 2008 contains significant measures to ensure that service users are involved in every aspect of their care.
It states that Service users must be treated with dignity and respect and that all care should be Person-centred. The care and treatment of service users must be appropriate, meet their needs, and reflect their preferences. Service users must give their consent and where they are unable to give consent because they lack capacity to do so, the registered person must

act in accordance with the mental capacity Act 2005. All treatments and care must be safe and service users must be protected from abuse or improper treatment. Premises and equipment must be fit for purpose and all nutritional and hydration needs must be met. The service must be well managed and should only employ fit and proper persons. All complaints must be handled appropriately and we have a duty of candor which states, we must act in an open and transparent way with relevant persons in relation to care and treatment provided to service users in carrying on a regulated activity.

The Care Standards Act 2000 and Essential standards for Quality and safety sets out what the service user can expect from their care provider and ensures providers ensure that they are given opportunities, encouragement and support to promote their independence. The Equality Act eliminates any unlawful discrimination, promotes equal opportunities and equality between protected groups.

The Mental Capacity Act 2005 sets out a framework for how decisions should be made in the best interests of someone who lacks mental capacity to make those decisions themselves. The service users living in my care home now have greater protection through legislation and consequently their rights to be involved fully in their daily living activities.

2.2

A manager is responsible for ensuring that staff plan and implement activities that meet the needs and preferences of service users. This includes: A clear understanding of the needs of the individuals using the service.

Supporting individuals to express their views

ensuring where individuals with complex needs or challenging behaviours for which staff are suitably trained. I support and guide the staff team to implement and plan our service user's daily living activities. The plans are individual to meet the service users needs and are devised with as much involvement of the service user as possible, where this is not possible our knowledge of previous preferences are used.

Care plans and their implementation are discussed in team meeting and in supervisions to ensure that all of my staff team understands how to safely and effectively support our service users. When a member of staff needs extra training I ensure that this is provided.

When a new member of staff is employed they always shadow for two weeks before they lone work. I ensure as far as possible that new staff shadow a senior team member for the first two weeks so that I can assess their performance and evaluate if the shadowing period needs to be extended. The service users are actively supported to have control over their daily living activities as far as possible.

2.3

The Department of Health visualizes personalisation applying to all individuals who use services in all care settings, and has equal resonance for those living in group settings where personalised approaches may still be less developed.

It is a necessity to consult service users to ensure they are central to decisions made about their lives ensuring an emphasis is placed on respect for the person's views and their right to self-determination and designing services around their specific needs.
It is difficult for me to ascertain the views of my service users because of their mental health. One service user is totally non-verbal
we have Person Centred Planning documentation in place for each service user, which gives consideration to many aspects of their lives, this documentation is used to device action plans and set any goals that we feel the service users might like to achieve. The PCP documents are completed and reviewed regularly by the Key worker and involve the service user as much as possible.

2.4

A manager's goal should be to achieve a high quality service. A manager needs to manage the monitoring and evaluation of the services provided.

To do this a manager may:
Obtain feedback from the service users
Obtain feedback from relatives and carers
Review how effective care plans have been implemented and whether goals identified have been met Obtain feedback from staff, particularly those with daily contact with the service users.

I regularly review the daily diaries and other records that are completed to ensure that all of the service user's daily living activities are fulfilled. This enables me to review the type of activity that they wish participating in and also whether it meets their needs and expectations and if they are working towards or meeting their goals. Implementing and overseeing regular monitoring and review of the systems and procedures which support group living and daily activities are part of my role as manager. as is having effective mechanisms to manage disagreements, conflicts and complaints. Performance can be measured against agreed standards to reveal when and where improvement is needed.

3 Be able to promote positive outcomes in a group living environment.

3.1

A manager needs to consider the kind of lifestyle the service enables individuals to have. The things that should be considered are: Does the service enable individuals to participate in everyday household and community activities? Does the service enable individuals to continue to develop their skills and experience thereby increasing the extent they can direct their own lives? Does the service enable individuals to increase and maintain their network of supportive friendships and relationships?

The main positive outcomes are the homes ability to maintain or prevent deterioration in the health of the service users and by us meeting their basic physical needs. The service users can be assisted or advised on personal hygiene and how to look presentable in appearance that promotes well-being and a feeling of pride and self worth. We ensure that nutritional needs are met by providing varied nutritional food and drink. The home is always clean, tidy and comfortable and provides a safe and secure environment for the service users and they benefit from having social contact and company. Service users have control over their daily routines and staffs are on hand to offer help and support when required.

The service users are listened to and have a say and some control over the services that they receive which promotes the feeling of being valued and respected.

Service users can benefit by being able to developing relationships with each other and the staff team which prevents them from feeling isolated and alone.

The home also encourages regular contact with family by facilitating telephone calls and visits.

3.2

It is a mistake to assume that all individuals living in a group setting will want to participate in group activities.

The individual service users should make their own informed choices of whether they wish to participate in group activities or not.

The benefits to individuals engaging in a range of activities promote mental stimulation and are important to health and well-being. Activities can stimulate the mind, build confidence and help form social bonds which could enable the service users to make new friends. Opportunities for meaningful activity can promote self-esteem, a feeling of wellbeing and mental health. It is important that individuals are able to freely choose whether they attend leisure and social activities, and the activities should contribute to the individual's personal goals, lead to positive outcomes and ensure that the service users lead fulfilling life. Physical activity has several benefits for the service users and can help improve sleep, maintain a healthy weight, build muscles, boost the immunity system and releases feel good endorphins. Mental activities such as word games or even friendly conversations give a positive boost to mental health, and encourage social interaction.

Group games such as Bingo can improve the ability to scan for information and can help short-term memory.

Socialisation through human contact is vital to well being and interactions with others are very meaningful and are integral to being happy and content with our lives. Social interaction is important to emotional well being and group activities such as doing a jigsaw puzzle can promote physical dexterity and creative thinking skills. By taking part in group activities improvements in the service users physical, mental and emotional functioning can all be enabled and their self confidence and feelings of self worth can be promoted

3.3

Individuals entering group living are often at a point of significant life transition. This is a time when their personal relationships may be fractured by losses of different kinds. It is important for each individual's well-being that their relationships with close friends and families are supported as best as possible.

It is very important to ensure that the service users maintain and develop relationships to prevent them from feeling or becoming isolated from family and friends.

3.4

Often in group living there may be times when individuals disagree with each other and conflicts can occur. It is important that all issues are dealt with in a timely and appropriate manner to ensure lasting damage is not caused.

If service users feel there is conflict with the service it is important that there are well established procedures to enable them to voice their concerns.

We ensure that our service users are supported by their key workers to voice any concerns and that the service users are aware that they can put in complaints and comments and our complaints / compliments procedures if explained to them clearly.

Sometime conflicts or issues with other service users can highlight issues that are affecting the service user, maybe from previous history in their lives and we encourage our service users to talk to us to see if there is anything we can do to assist them.

By encouraging an atmosphere of mutual respect within the care home conflicts are few and far between, but when there is conflict it is my role to deal with it whether they are between staff or the service users.

I arbitrate between the parties involved and keep the lines of communication open and I listen to everyone viewpoints. I must be objective and impartial and be willing to negotiate and make compromises. I find that by keeping everyone calm and listening to their viewpoint most conflicts can be dealt with in an amicable fashion. If the situation cannot be dealt with by myself the human resource department is asked to step in.

4 Be able to manage a positive group living environment.

4.1

A good manager should lead on good practice to ensure staff in turn ensures that individuals / service user's needs are met. A consideration is whether the working patterns of the staff are contributing effectively to meeting the needs of the service users. My care home provides twenty four hour care to effectively cover the shifts that are needed to support the service users I have a Rota that is compiled monthly. The staff team is made up of four full time staff and three one to one staff.

Continuity of care is not only important for the service user's but also for the staff team. It can be both rewarding and create job satisfaction to have long term relationships with individuals and their families. It can be emotionally rewarding and also makes more sense in understanding the service users especially when they have complex needs. I believe by having a dedicated team appropriate and effective care can be given. A stable and experienced staff team is more confident in how to support the service users and the service users seem to be more at ease when receiving care.

4.2

A good manager should review working staff patterns regularly to ensure that systems are working effectively. This process can take place in a number of ways, a few are:
How individual member of staff perform during supervision
Discussing effectiveness at team meetings
Getting feedback from CQC inspectors
Feedback from service users

4.3

A good manager should ensure that they have adequate staffing levels at all times and that staff are adequately trained. It is also important to ensure staffs feel valued and part of a team and works well together and is well informed thus maintaining a happy and dedicated staff team.

It is also important to have a contingency plan for staffing issues and a succession plan for the future.
My aim is to develop a confident, capable and well- trained workforce which can empower the service users to have as much independence and choice as possible. With the purpose of enabling them to stay healthy and active to promote their health and well-being. As a care home we must have a work force that is equipped with the right skills to deliver safe and high quality services which focus on supporting self direction, dignity, independence and choice,

Recruitment and retention of quality staff is crucial to ensure that people with the right potential are recruited and are retained to ensure continuity for the service users. In order to continue meeting the changing needs and preferences of the service user's staff need to be encouraged and assisted to develop their knowledge and skills. PL offer a high standard of induction and training opportunities and has a commitment to supporting their staff teams with ongoing refresher training. PL also endeavor to identify and develop staff that have the potential to progress within the organisation and eventually fill key leadership positions in the workplace. This was the case with my own development within PL, I started as a support worker and was given the opportunity to be a senior and gain QCF level 5. I have recently become a manager. By nurturing and developing promising members of staff PL increases the availability of experienced and capable employees that are prepared to assume supervisory and managerial roles as they become available.

My training plan ensures that staff attend induction training when they first start employment and that all mandatory training is attended by all of the staff. To ensure that we have a well-trained team and to enable us to provide a better service, all staff are expected to attain a health and social care diploma Level 2 if they so wish. Those identified as showing promise are offered the opportunity to do level 3 as is the case with several of the staff team here at my care home.

As the registered manager I need to monitor the staff team and identify the skills mix required within the care home to ensure that we deliver and continue to deliver a high quality service, and comply with current legislation.

It is important that I keep up to date with proposed and current legislations and that I ensure that my staff team has the right mix of skills, competencies, qualifications, experience and knowledge to meet the service users needs.

4.4

Staff should be trained and educated through supervision and staff meetings to be aware of the importance of professional boundaries, all staff need to understand there are considerable risks to both individuals using the service and staff where boundaries are threatened or crossed.
For the home to be a caring home staff need to build a rapport with the service users and they should ensure that they establish and maintain appropriate professional boundaries in the relationships between themselves and the service users. Boundaries define the limits of behaviour, which allow a professional carer and an individual to engage safely in a supportive caring relationship. These boundaries are based upon trust, respect and the appropriate use of power and must focus solely upon meeting the needs of the Service user. Should the focus move towards meeting the employee's own needs this would be an unacceptable abuse of power and staff need to respect the boundary around their relationships with the service users. They must not enter into relationships that exploit the service users, sexually, physically, emotionally, socially or in any other manner. They must not develop relationships which compromise their professional judgment and objectivity and/or give rise to advantageous or disadvantageous treatment of the service user. Staff must not try to influence service users, other members of staff or other individuals living in the home by impressing their own beliefs and values on them. In some situations the fine line between good and bad practice may not always be obvious or clear. On occasions a member of staff may develop an attachment towards a particular service user, while this may be a natural progression of a professional relationship, the staff member should ensure it does not lead to a breach of the professional boundaries.

I encourage my staff team to talk about the service users during supervision and I offer advice and support if they are unsure about the nature of a developing professional relationship with a service user.

I conduct regular monitoring and review to ensure my company's policies, procedures and guidelines, regarding boundaries are being upheld.

4.5

Group living environments are unique settings, with complex relationships between everyone. One should consider relationships between the service users, between service users and staff and between staff members.

A good manager should be aware of the group dynamics in their environment. They should ensure the staff team works well together and they collaborate and share information. It is important to be aware of the dynamics between service users and be constantly aware of any changes.
Group dynamics refers to a system of behaviours and psychological processes occurring within or between social groups. A group is two or more people who are interacting with one another to achieve a common goal or purpose which is striving to achieve a shared outcome. The group should provide each member with a level of acceptance, listen to their views and provide a forum for the membership to express their opinions. Each member's opinion may of course be consistent or inconsistent with the group's aims or goals. Because every individual has their own personality and views, the aim should be to mould the group into a cohesive team which is working for a common goal. Disagreement and dissention among group members is only to be expected and is a normal path that all groups traverse. For an effective and dynamic group to evolve, members need to recognise the interdependence model exhibited by its members and find ways to deal with them for the overall good. The group needs to be open and honest and share information because communication is the key to successful interaction.

Providing a positive group living environment starts with good management of the home and by maintaining the environment to a high standard. It is also promoted by ensuring and training staff to give choice and respect the preferences of the service users, and by encouraging the service users to remain as independent as possible and by ensuring adequate monitoring of staff through regular supervisions and appraisals to ensure staff are aware of good practices and that they adhere to them. A good method of assuring the effectiveness of the group is for the members to show common courtesies to each other by giving support and encouragement to each other. I try to promote an environment that encourages openness and idea sharing among the group where everyone has a valid point of view.

Good training can improve my staff teams communication skills, both verbal and non-verbal and can aid them with working within the group
The service users participate in group activities in different ways and at different levels

because of several factors which include their individual capabilities, the physical environment, the psychological atmosphere, their own personality and how they feel about taking part and interacting with others.

4.6

A good manager should always review the different resources available to them and consider how these resources support positive outcomes for the individual service users. It is very important to manage the care homes resources to ensure that we remain within budget and continue to be commercially viable.
I have to manage the budget to ensure that staffing levels are within the requirements of regulations and that they meet the service user's individual needs, and at the same time stay within my budget.

CU3087 Lead Person Centred Practice

1 Understand the theory and principles that underpin person centred practice.

1.1

All patients should be treated as individuals and their care should reflect this. Person-centred practice is an approach that puts the client at the centre of their care. Their care is structured around their individual needs. It involves them in making decisions about things that affect them. Person centred planning is crucial to providing quality care and support. It helps professional care and support workers find out what is important to the person they support and enables services to be built around what matters most to that individual. When you get to know the client well, you can provide care that is more specific to their needs and therefore provide better care. By promoting and facilitating greater client responsibility, clients are more likely to engage in treatment decisions, feel supported to make behavioural changes and feel empowered to self manage.
The 'person centred approach' is a model of practice which puts the individual's personal wishes and interests at the heart of every aspect of their care. Person centred practice endeavours to form a partnership with the service user to develop a plan of care which can be developed over time to suit every aspect of their needs.

Person centred care is 'user focussed' and is designed to preserve independence and promote individual choice. This leads to greater autonomy and inclusion and builds solid relationships with the service users and their families.

Broadly speaking, Person centred care is about preserving individuality and promoting personal diversity. It is about building an in depth but professional relationship with a service user and counteracting the effects of institutionalisation on the individual.

1.2

With person-centred practice the main person is the client. The service would be organised for their individual needs concerning their personal care and well being. It should cover all aspects of health and social care. They must include the following:

Ensuring that the client is treated with dignity and respect.
Enabling them to achieve as much independence as possible.
Ensuring that the client has choices.
Ensuring that the client is treated as an individual.
Ensuring that their rights are maintained.

Person-centred practice gives the individual the control over aspects of their life, making decisions and overcoming barriers to participate in every day events. This will give the client a feeling of well being.
The main approach to person centred care within my own job role is based around the use of an extensive personal care plan. The person centred care plan is integral to providing a fully optimised set of support plans which set out a detailed and easy to follow plan of care. The plans are broken down into sub sections depending on the service user's individual needs and preferences. This allows for systematic detailed reviews on a monthly basis and individual amendments and changes as soon as the need is identified. Upon admission, All residents have a new care plan which is written based on information gathered from a Pre - Assessment (which ascertains whether an individual's needs can be met from an institutional perspective), Talking with the resident themselves, Liaising with family or carers and also analysing any specific medical notes. This information allows a set of support plans to be drafted as soon as a service user is admitted. All staff will then make entries into a daily support plan which provides a chronological narration of the individual's day to day life within the home. This includes all information about daily life, health issues, mental well-being, personal care, nutrition, sleeping habits, interactions with other individuals. It is this information which acts as the baseline for future development of the overall plan of care.

During systematic review of each individual support plan, the daily support plan reference is used to contrast information about the individual with the support plan and ensure that it is 'valid' for example laying out a plan of care which caters for that persons needs effectively. It may also be identified through the monthly reviewing that additional support plans are needed for issues such as continence, expression of sexual needs or health & safety issues.

Other input into the care plan comes from an annual review of all support plans with the service user's family or designated advocate. As within a mental health care setting it is not always possible for an individual with diminished cognition to specifically discuss their own support plan outright, we ensure that the family are also happy with all aspects of the plan of care and ask them to countersign on behalf of the resident. This of course promotes further inclusion of family etc. in a service user's care and helps to develop an extended professional relationship.

A person centred care plan is only as good as the information contributed to them from the service users and family, the historical data can be added from previous notes we have on individuals but doesn't always express wishes and views.

1.3

The government continues to provide policies to enable patients to be promoted with the choice of their care by promoting legislations. Legislations as follows:

Department of Health 2009 has proposals to broaden the range of providers and introduce more competition into care services. This enables the clients to be able to go to their local surgeries instead of wasting time at the local hospital. The Health Foundation 2012 reports that implementing "no decision about me, without me" required a considerable change in culture and practice in care settings. This has enabled the clients to be consulted regarding their everyday care needs.

MHA guidelines on the approach to person centred care and practice endeavour to uphold the core values of promoting the individuals inclusion in decisions about their care and life within the home. The company's policy on care planning has been written and amended in accordance with various acts of legislation issued by the department of health and also The Care standards Act (2000).

All Plans of Care from admission to discharge are written in line with MHA's Values Statement and also adhere to all criteria detailed in The Care Standards Act. This covers all of a resident's health (both physical and mental) and personal & social care needs. The current draft of the policy reflects the core values of person centred care, with a strong emphasis on including both the resident and also their family or appointed advocate in all of its aspects.

The policy for care planning details extensive criteria of what must be included in the residents care plan in order to comply with the national minimum standards outlined in the Care Standards Act. This is arranged in a specifically structured order that ultimately allows for all information to be easily accessed, monitored and reviewed.

More importantly, this allows anyone who knows the structure of the care plan to be able to familiarise themselves with any aspect of a residents plan of care and apply the information to their own practice. As each section of the care plan is systematically reviewed and updated to ensure that it is compliant with legislation and internal policy, this means that individual's needs are outlined in detail and coupled with relevant outcomes. This in turn means that a new member of staff can be easily directed to relevant sections of the care plan and that the information provided allows them to provide care to the agreed legal standard.

1.4

Person centred practice can inform how consent is established. All staff that work for PL are given training in how to obtain consent from individual clients and the different ways that we can obtain consent. Person-centred practice may include that the individual needs an advocate (IMCA) or social worker to act on their behalf. They must be afforded this choice. This will enable the client to be treated with the values and beliefs they wish. If the client has difficulty communicating there are various ways to communicate. If the client is hard of hearing, sign language may be used. If the client speaks English as a second language, an interpreter may be used. This is all arranged around the client's person-centred practice and must be included in their every day care. If they are not capable of giving consent, then they must have a mental capacity assessment and their care must be centred on their best interests. They are given an informed choice.

Person centred practice is based around establishing effective, personalised means of communication with service users. Through day to day interactions with residents, strategies are developed to build up effective lines of communication with those individuals. The important consideration, especially in a Mental Health care setting is that resident's capacity to communicate is highly variable, therefore establishment of consent can often be somewhat problematic. Each resident has their own individual ways of communicating, in my own personal experience this can be as simple as understanding a gesture or a behaviour with the individual at that particular time.

Approaching this aspect of care from a person centred perspective means that from the first instance of admission, an in depth assessment has already been made to gather all available information about that person for initial development of the support plans. However, the most effective means of establishing communication comes from one to one interaction with the resident.

Communication is about taking the time to provide the right reassurance to that person and making sure that they have ample opportunity to express themselves.

There is generally always a way to establish consent for most things, with very little instances where there is no communication at all. Person centred care informs the way in which consent is established by promoting the building of relations and taking time to understand a person's individuality, behaviours and preferences.

1.5

The aim is to give the client as much control over their lives as possible. It may only be a small change for example we have one client who can't swallow tablets and requires them crushed, we spoke to the doctor and got consent for the client to crush his medication. This enabled the service user to carry on with his everyday life without fear of medication times and swallowing concerns. Person-centred practice may be on a larger scale for example our mental health patients will receive direct payments into their bank accounts and they choose what holistic treatments they would like with support from staff.

Because person centred practice emphasises the empowerment of the individual in decisions regarding the care they receive, there is a constant drive towards improving that persons quality of life. Prior to the widespread introduction of Person centred practice, treatment of service users in care was based on the medical model, allowing their condition or disability to define them. The medical model worked on the presumption that an individual could not be deemed as able to be independent or make decisions for themselves before that condition was overcome. With a progressive illness such as dementia, this model of care raises many issues regarding detrimental effects on that individual's mental and spiritual well being, due to the simple fact it removes an individual's personal choice. If a condition by its nature has no chance of improving, this means there is also little hope for that individual of having any further control of their life. By its own definition. Person centred practice reverses this by putting the individual first and allowing the most prominent level of input to be based on that persons individuals preferences and wishes.

The positive effects in an individual's life are counteracting conditions associated with depression and personal withdrawal. These can be issues such as feeling a lack of progression in their life, stigmatisation regarding their illness and delusions of over dependency; all of which were common during the institutional use of the medical model in the social care sector.

As long as an individual is defined as having a level of independence, they are given the means by which to express themselves in whatever capacity they are able. The input into their care begins from when they are first admitted and their plan of care begins. Having this baseline in place allows for an increase in more varied, genuine life experiences even whilst in care. In certain cases, dependant on previous life conditions this can allow for improvement in the individuals life, further inclusion in community events and the forming of new relationships with others.

2 Be able to lead a person-centred practice.

2.1

As part of the senior team it is my responsibility to work with clients and their families to establish their personal history. All clients have their individual care plan which show the client's medical history and care needs. This will enable the care worker when caring for the client to have better knowledge both of conditions the client has and their preferences. As a senior team member I would monitor the care worker to ensure they are abiding by the client's wishes and needs for example if the Client has OCD and is obsessive with putting their clothes in order; the care worker would work alongside the patient and ensure that this is done.

2.2 &2.3

Care staffs are given a weekly rota and the care workers feed back any information that the client requires, this can be fed back to the other Care workers that work other shift. This is also documented in the client's care plan. As a senior team member I also observe this when I monitor the care workers whilst doing spot checks and supervisions. Support others to work with individuals to review approaches to meet individuals' needs and preferences. Observation and discussion will enable us to work together as a team and ensure that the client's needs are being met.

2.4

One way of reviewing approaches is by supervision. When I complete supervisions with the care workers I ask them if there is any training that they feel they need to enable them to do their jobs properly and correctly. This improves their quality of work. They tell me what they feel is effective whilst carrying out their roles and it is an opportunity to see if there are alternative ways that can be tried in practice. Individual's needs may adapt and change over time through regular updates of care plans and involvement of all teams members we can devise new systems and ways of working within legal guidelines to support the individuals we support.

3 Be able to lead the implementation of active participation of individuals.

3.1

The main essential part of Lead person-centred practice is to include the client as an active participant in their every day care. If the client is not included then it is not person-centred practice. We have Social Workers, Occupational Therapists and district nurses who set plans which are individual to each client. This enables the clients to have a feeling of self worth and achievement when the goals are met.
The principle of active participation is one of the cornerstones of person centred care. It is in direct opposition of the ideas behind the now obsolete Medical Model for the provision of care. This is due to the fact that the key principle literally includes the individual by putting them in the centre of all decisions that are made about their provision of care. Although in terms of practical application, the amount a person can input into the care planning process can be extremely variable depending on their cognitive ability and communication skills; however active participation can always be achieved in some capacity.

Building up a relationship with a resident and understanding their abilities leads to the development of more effective forms of communication and therefore a greater platform for the facilitation of active participation. This is especially relevant when working with people who have limited ability to communicate, as establishing effective routes of communication not only increases interaction with the resident; it also contributes to the ongoing development of support plans.

Active participation does not just apply to the individual resident, but also to family members and appointed advocates. Through my own job role, there is an annual review of all support plans with next of kin or other designated individuals. Due to the nature of the conditions of many of the residents at PL, this is one of the most productive means of support plan development from external input. This is also especially relevant during pre - assessment as there is often very little known about a resident prior to admission. Focussing on increasing the input of residents and their families in their care not only aids the individualisation of support provided, but also promotes inclusion.

Although all residents are different, the minority of people within PL are deemed as not having capacity. This means that it is often not possible to be able to involve that person in more major decision making; this usually falls to the next of kin. The process of active participation commonly comes from acts of inclusion in day to day living tasks which have to be duly risk assessed and are normally conducted by activities staff. This can be something as small as walking to the shop to by a newspaper or visiting friends or relatives away from the home.

Even in the smallest capacity, any act of active inclusion is always of therapeutic benefit to an individual service user. Building relationships from a person centred approach with residents, there is always ways for them to develop new interests and build friendships. Promoting active participation allows staff to find the opportunity to facilitate this. Making an individual an active partner in their care it is possible for anyone in some capacity regardless of their cognitive impairment or condition to have active participation.

3.2 & 3.3

To implement systems that promote active participation and support risk assessments we must endeavour to include the service user in all aspects of their care needs including care planning and risk assessments. To enable us to achieve this we need a good history of the client in our care, this may come from the service user, their family or a mixture of both.

An assessment usually carried out initially with a social worker will highlight the potential and abilities of the clients. It will encompass their needs, wishes and preferences. This will then be re- visited over the course of the client staying in our service usually on an annual basis. This allows for the check for change element to identify if needs have changed.

Person centred care means asking the client want they want and keep asking them on a regular basis as wishes change and what was wanted once may not apply every time.

Person centred care means respect of peoples individuality in respect to culture, beliefs, age, gender, ethnicity or other characteristics.

Risk assessments should be made and checked regularly to enable the individual to actively participate in their own care. Only because an activity is deemed risky or unwise by some doesn't mean that there are no benefits to the person wanting to achieve the activity.

Regular supervisions will enable the senior team to monitor performance in all aspects of individual care, also allowing for feedback from team members to highlight any shortfalls they feel are occurring. The supervision process will also allow for identification of training required, and input from clients in their own care needs.

CU3119 Understand Safeguarding of Children and Young People for Those Working in the Adult Sector

1 Understand the policies, procedures and practices for safe working with children and young people.

1.1

There is no single piece of legislation that covers 'child protection' or 'safeguarding' in the UK but a number of laws that are continually being amended, updated or revoked. The Children's Act 1989 provides a comprehensive framework for the care and protection of children. It centres on the welfare of children up to their 18th birthday. It defines parental responsibility and encourages partnership working with parents. Interagency co-operation is encouraged. The Children's Act 2004 supplemented the 1989 Act and reinforced the message that all organisations working with children have a duty in helping safeguard and promote the welfare of children.
Some legislation we need to be aware of to ensure safe working with Children and young people are:

Protection of Children Act (1999), Data Protection Act (1998), The Children Act (Every Child Matters (ECM) 2004, Safeguarding Vulnerable Groups Act 2006, Childcare Act 2006, Mental Capacity Act (2006), Deprivation of Liberty Safeguards, Human Rights Act (1998), Equalities Act (2010), Protection of Children Act, Working Together to Safeguard Children 2006 (revised 2010), The Protection of Children in England: A progress report 2009. Independent safeguarding Authority, The Children's Act 1989.

The Children Act 1989, implemented for the most part on 14 October 1991, introduced comprehensive changes to legislation in England and Wales affecting the welfare of children. The Act:

reinforces the autonomy of families through definition of parental responsibility; provides for support from local authorities, in particular for families whose children are in need; and legislates to protect children who may be suffering or are likely to suffer significant harm.

Annual reports on the progress of the Act were published by the Children Act Advisory Committee until 1997, but the Committee was then abolished. The Government is required to publish a report on the Act every 5 years, and statistics on its application are also available. There are also research reports on the operation of the Act (see Aldgate & Statham, 2001).

The main aims of the Act are:
to bring together private and public law in one framework; to achieve a better balance between protecting children and enabling parents to challenge state intervention; to encourage greater partnership between statutory authorities and parents, to promote the use of voluntary arrangements;
to restructure the framework of the courts to facilitate management of family proceedings.

What changed with the Children Act 2004?
Following the death of eight-year old Victoria Climbié in 2000, the Government asked Lord Laming to conduct an inquiry (Laming, 2003) to help decide whether to introduce new legislation and guidance to improve the child protection system in England. The Government's response was the Keeping children safe report (DfES, DH and Home Office, 2003) and the Every Child Matters green paper (DfES, 2003), which led to the Children Act 2004. The Children Act 2004 does not replace or even amend much of the Children Act 1989. It covers England and Wales in separate sections. The Act:
creates the post of Children's Commissioner for England.
Places a duty on local authorities to appoint a director of children's services and an elected lead member for children's services, who is ultimately accountable for the delivery of services. The government published revised statutory guidance relating to the two posts in April 2012 (DfES, 2012) places a duty on local authorities and their partners (including the police, health service providers and the youth justice system) to co-operate in promoting the wellbeing of children and young people and to make arrangements to safeguard and promote the welfare of children states the creation of the new Local Safeguarding Children Boards (replacing the non-statutory Area Child Protection Committees) and gives them functions of investigation and review (sections 13 and 14), which they use to review all child deaths in their area updates the legislation on physical punishment (section 58) by limiting the use of the defence of reasonable punishment so that it can no longer be used when people are charged with the offences against a child of wounding, actual or grievous bodily harm or cruelty. Therefore any injury sustained by a child which is serious enough to warrant a charge of assault occasioning actual bodily harm cannot be considered to be as the result of reasonable punishment.

CHILDCARE ACT 2006,

The Childcare Act has four parts: duties on local authorities in England (Part 1); duties on local authorities in Wales (Part 2); regulation and inspection arrangements for childcare providers in England (Part 3); and general provisions (Part 4). Key provisions are as follows.

Sections 1-5 require local authorities and their NHS and Jobcentre Plus partners to work together to improve the outcomes of all children up to 5 and reduce inequalities between them, by ensuring early childhood services are integrated to maximise access and benefits to families - underpinning a Sure Start Children's Centre for every community

Sections 6, 8-11 & 13 require local authorities to assess the local childcare market and to secure sufficient childcare for working parents. Childcare will only be deemed sufficient if meets the needs of the community in general and in particular those families on lower incomes and those with disabled children. Local authorities take the strategic lead in their local childcare market, planning, supporting and commissioning childcare. Local authorities will not be expected to provide childcare direct but will be expected to work with local private, voluntary and independent sector providers to meet local need.

Section 7 re-enacts the duty for local authorities to secure a free minimum amount of early learning and care for all 3 and 4 year olds whose parents want it.

Section 12 extends the existing duty to provide information to parents, to ensure parents and prospective parents can access the full range of information they may need for their children right through to their 20th birthday. Local authorities will be required to ensure that this service is available to all parents and that it is pro-active in reaching those parents who might otherwise have difficulty accessing the information service.

Sections 39-48 introduce the Early Years Foundation Stage (EYFS) which will build on and bring together the existing Birth to Three Matters, Foundation Stage and national standards for under 8s day care and childminding. The EYFS will support providers in delivering high quality integrated early education and care for children from birth to age 5.

Sections 31-98 reform and simplify the framework for the regulation of childcare and early education to reduce bureaucracy and focus on raising quality and standards. All providers caring for children from birth to the 31 August following their fifth birthday will be required to register on the Early Years register and deliver the Early Years Foundation Stage (unless exceptionally exempted). Childcare settings providing for children from the 1 September following their fifth birthday up to the age of eight must register on the compulsory part of the Ofsted Childcare Register (unless they are exempt.) The Act introduced certain requirements that all providers who are registering on the Ofsted Childcare Register will need to meet some of which are provided for in the Act but most of which are laid down in associated Regulations made under the Act.. Those childcare providers who are not obliged to register on the compulsory part of the Ofsted Childcare Register can choose to join the voluntary part of the Register. These providers will also need to meet certain requirements, which are laid down in Regulations made under the Act.

Sections 99-101 allow for the collection of information about young children to inform funding and support the local authority duties under the Act.

Every Child Matters
This is a Government Green Paper, the 'Every Child Matters' was published at the same time as the government's response to the report into the death of Victoria Climbie. Every Child Matters built on plans already in place to prevent the abuse of children, it focused on: Increasing the focus on supporting families and carers

Ensuring necessary intervention takes place before children reach crisis point Addressing the underlying problems identified in the report into the death of Victoria Climbie weak accountability and poor integration Ensuring that the people working with children are valued, rewarded and trained

After consultation, the government published Every Child Matter: Next Steps and passed the Children Act 2004, providing the legislation which could support the development of more effective, accessible services which focused on the needs of children, young people and their families. Every Child Matters: Change for Children (2004) outlines the government's approach to the well-being of children and young people from birth to age 19, or 24 for those with disabilities. The aim is that every child, whatever their background or circumstances should have the support they need to:

Be healthy, stay safe, enjoying and achieving, make a positive contribution, and achieve economic well-being.
Any organisations involved with providing services to children must genuinely work in partnership and share information, to protect children and young people from harm and help them achieve what they want in life. Emphasis is placed on the idea that, for each child to fulfil their potential, there must be a greater deal of co-operation, not only between Government agencies, but also between schools, GPs, Sports organisations and the Voluntary and Community sector. The Every Child Matters initiative provides a detailed framework for working with children within multi- agency partnerships. The themes covering health, safety, achievement of well- being and positive contribution making. One of the criticisms of services had been the failure of professionals to understand each other's roles or to work together in a multi- disciplinary manner and the ECM initiative sought to change this.

As we are a provider that carries out a regulated service we have to be registered with Care Quality Commission. We have to take into account the Care Quality Commission Essential standards quality and safety, which is a guide to help providers of health and social care to comply with the Health and Social Care Act 2008 (Regulated Activities) Regulation 2010 and the Care Quality Commission (Registration) Regulation 2009. These regulations describe the essential standards of quality and safety that people who use health and adult care services have a right to expect. The Care Quality Commission will continuously monitor our service to ensure that we are meeting the essential standards and if they have any concerns that at any time we was not meeting the essential standards of quality and safety they will act quickly, working closely with commissioners and others, and using their enforcement powers to bring about improvements if our service was poor or to prevent us from carrying out regulated activities.

A person who uses care services can be protected from abuse or the risk of abuse when service providers comply with these regulations they will:

Take action to identify and prevent abuse from happening in their service, Respond appropriately when it is suspected that abuse has occurred or there is a risk of occurring, Ensure that Government and local guidance about safeguarding people from abuse is accessible to all staff and out into practice, Make sure that the use of restraint is always appropriate, reasonable, proportionate and justifiable to the individual, Only use de-escalation or restraint in a way that respects dignity and protects human rights. Where possible respect the preferences of people who uses the services, Understand how diversity, beliefs and values of people who uses services may be influence the identification, prevention and response to safeguarding concerns, Protect others from negative effect of any behaviour by people who use the service, Where applicable, only use Deprivation of Liberty Safeguarding when it is in the best interests of people who uses the service and in accordance with the Mental Capacity Act 2005.

2 Understand how to respond to evidence or concerns that a child or young person has been abused or harmed.

2.1

Abuse and neglect are forms of maltreatment of a child. Somebody may abuse or neglect a child by inflicting harm, or by failing to act to prevent it. Children may be abused in a family or in an institutional or community setting, by somebody they know or more rarely by a stranger, for example, via the internet. They may be abused by adults or other children.

There are several different forms of abuse I will highlight some here.
Physical Abuse.

This may involve hitting, shaking, poisoning, burning, scalding, suffocating or any cause of physical harm to a child. Physical harm may also be caused by a parent or care giver fabricating the symptoms of, or deliberately inducing illness in a child.

some Physical signs of physical abuse are:
Unexplained bruising
Multiple bruising to upper arms and outer thighs
Human bite marks
Fractures
Scalds

Some symptoms/signs and behaviours of physical abuse are:
Temper Outbursts
Fear of parent being approached
Depression
Withdrawn
Improbable excuses to explain injuries
Wearing inappropriate clothes for weather conditions to hide injuries Running away all the time
Fear of medical help or examination
Aggression towards others
Fear of physical contact shrinking back if touched
Self-destructive tendencies
Fear of suspected abuser being contacted

Sexual Abuse
Sexual abuse involves forcing or enticing a child or young person to take part in sexual activities. The activities may involve physical contact, including rape and oral sex or non-penetrative acts such as masturbation, kissing, rubbing and touching outside of clothing. They may also include non-contact activities such as involving children in looking at, or the production of images, watching sexual activities or encouraging children to act in sexually inappropriate ways and grooming them in preparation for abuse. Sexual abuse is not only perpetrated by males, women can also commit acts of sexual abuse, as can other children.

some signs of Sexual Abuse:
Bruising or bleeding near genital area
Pain or itching around genital area
Discomfort when walking or sitting
Pregnancy
Sexual transmitted disease
Stomach pains
Vaginal discharge or infection

Some of the symptoms/indicators and behaviours of sexual abuse are: Nightmares
Bed wetting
Easting problems
Aggressive or withdrawn
Drug/substance abuse
Unexplained sources of money or items
Being overly affectionate or knowledgeable in a sexual way inappropriate to the child's age
Medical problems such as chronic itching, pain in the genitals, venereal diseases Depression, self-harm, suicide attempts, running away, overdoses, anorexia Personality changes such as becoming insecure or clingy.
Regressing to younger behaviour patterns for example thumb sucking Becoming isolated or

withdrawn
Inability to concentrate
Lack of trust or fear of someone they know well, for example not wanting to be alone with the babysitter, Fear of clothing being removed
Suddenly drawing sexually explicit pictures

Emotional Abuse
Emotional abuse is the persistent maltreatment of a child that causes severe and adverse effects on the child's emotional development. It may involve conveying to children that they are worthless, unloved or inadequate. It may include not giving the child opportunity to express themselves, making fun of what they say or how they communicate or deliberately silencing them. It may involve serious bullying, including cyber bullying, causing children frequently to feel frightened or in danger, or the exploitation or corruption of children. Some level of emotional abuse is involved in all types of maltreatment of children, though it may occur alone.

Signs of emotional abuse may include:
Failure to thrive
Development issues
Parents display little or no affection
Receive little attention from parents

Symptoms/indicators and behaviours of emotional abuse may include:

Self-harm such as cutting
Fear of parent being approached
Speech disorders which develop suddenly
Developmental delay re emotional progress
Physical, mental and emotional development lags
Continual self-depreciation ('I'm stupid, I'm ugly etc') Overreaction to mistakes
Extreme fear of any new situation
Neurotic behaviour (rocking, hair twisting, self-mutilation) Extremes of passivity or aggression

Neglect
Neglect is the persistent failure to meet the child's basic physical and/or psychological needs, likely to result in the impairment of the child's health or development. Neglect may result in pregnancy as a result of maternal substance abuse. Once a child is born, neglect may involve a parent or care giver failing to: Provide adequate food, clothing or shelter

Protect a child from emotional or physical harm or danger
Ensure adequate supervision, including the use of inadequate care provision Ensure access to adequate to appropriate medical care or treatment It may also include neglect of a Childs basic emotional needs.

signs of neglect may include:
Child dirty or smelly
Child constantly hungry
Child underweight
Inappropriately dressed for the weather

Symptoms/indicators and behaviours of neglect may be:
Constantly tired
Having few friends
Being left alone/unsupervised
Constant hunger
Poor personal hygiene
Poor state of clothing
Emaciation
Untreated medical problems
No social relationships
Compulsive scavenging
Destructive tendencies

Bullying

Under the Children Act 1989 an incident of bullying should be treated as child protection when a child is suffering or likely to suffer significant harm under the Equalities Act 2010 public bodies, which includes schools must address and eliminate unlawful discrimination, harassment and victimisation. Bullying is not always easy to recognise and can take a number of forms. They can be bullying attacks that are physical (pushing, hitting, pinching and other forms of or violence) or the can be verbal (name calling, sarcasm, spreading rumours, persistent teasing, ridiculing, humiliating).

Signs of bullying can include:
Depression
Low self esteem
Shyness
Isolation
Poor academic achievement
Threatened or attempted suicide

Symptoms/indicators and behaviours of a bullied child may include: Coming home with cuts and bruises
Torn clothes
Losing dinner money
Being moody or bad tempered
Asking for stolen possessions to be replaced
Falling out with previously good friends

Wanting to avoid leaving home
Aggression with siblings
Sleep problems
Anxiety
Being less well at school
Becoming quiet and withdrawn

2.2

Recognising child abuse is not easy and it is not our responsibility to decide if abuse has taken place or not, but we do have a responsibility and duty of care to act in order that the appropriate agencies can investigate and take any necessary action to protect a child.

The DFES guidance entitled 'What to do if you're worried a child is being abused – summary' advises that you should: Be familiar with and follow your organisation's procedures and protocols for promoting and safeguarding the welfare of children in your area, and know who to contact in your organisation to express concerns about a child's welfare. Remember that an allegation of child abuse or neglect or neglect may lead to a criminal investigation, so don't do anything that may jeopardise a police investigation. Ensure that you know who is responsible for making referrals and if it is your responsibility know who to contact in police, health, education, school and children's social care to express concerns about a child's welfare. When referring a child to children's social services you should consider and include any information on the child's development needs and their parents/carers capacity to respond to these needs within the context of their wider family environment. See the child and ascertain their wishes and feelings as part of considering what action to take in relation to the child's welfare. Communicate with the child in a way that is appropriate to their age and understanding, especially if the child is disabled and for children whose first language is not English. Depending on the substance and seriousness of the concerns you may require advice from the police or children's social care to ensure you do not jeopardise the safety of the child or any subsequent investigation. It is important to reassure the child however you must not promise confidentiality. Record full information about the child including their name, address, gender, date of birth, name/s of person/s with parental responsibility (for consent purposes) and primary carer if different. Keep this information up to date. Record all concerns, discussions about the child, the decisions that were made and reasons for those decisions in writing. The child's records should include an up to date account, and details of the lead worker in the relevant agencies, for example social worker, teacher or health visitor. Knowing how damaging abuse is to children it is up to the adults around them to take responsibility for stopping it. If you are concerned or a child tells you about abuse you must report it immediately. The following can be contacted through your telephone directory:

Police, Social Services, Samaritans, NSPCC, ChildLine, Parentline.

2.3

In 1991 the United Nations Convention on the Rights if the Child 1989 was sanctioned in the UK and included the following rights for children:

The right to protection from abuse.
The right to express their views.
The right to be listened to.
The right to care and services for disabled children or children living away from home.
The right to protection from any form of discrimination.
The right to receive and share information as long as that information is not damaging to others.   The right to freedom of religion.
The right to education.

The law has now given children a voice and as stated in the Children's Act 2004, the best interest of the child is paramount in all considerations of welfare (convention of the rights of the child 1989 - Article 3). Children should be protected from all forms of violence (Convention of the rights of the child 1989 – Article 19) Children should be separated from their parents if they have been abused or neglected (Convention of the rights of the child 1989 – Article 19). This can cause tensions with child's parents as this is irrespective of what they think. The child does have a right to confidentiality during investigations but the care worker should also make it clear that they have a duty of care to protect and safeguard the child which may mean sharing information with others, on a strictly need to know basis.

1. Understand the policies, procedures and practices for safe working with children and young people.

There is no single piece of legislation that covers 'child protection' or 'safeguarding' in the UK but a number of laws that are continually being amended, updated or revoked. The Children's Act 1989 provides a comprehensive framework for the care and protection of children. It centres on the welfare of children up to their 18th birthday. It defines parental responsibility and encourages partnership working with parents. Interagency co-operation is encouraged. The Children's Act 2004 supplemented the 1989 Act and reinforced the message that all organisations working with children have a duty in helping safeguard and promote the welfare of children.

Some legislation we need to be aware of to ensure safe working with Children and young people are:

Children Act (1989)
Protection of Children Act (1999)
Data Protection Act (1998)
The Children Act (Every Child Matters (ECM) 2004
Safeguarding Vulnerable Groups Act 2006
Childcare Act 2006
Mental Capacity Act (2006)
Deprivation of Liberty Safeguards
Human Rights Act (1998)
Equalities Act (2010)
Protection of Children Act
Working Together to Safeguard Children 2006 (revised 2010)

The Protection of Children in England: A progress report 2009. Independent safeguarding Authority

The Children's Act 1989
The Children Act 1989, implemented for the most part on 14 October 1991, introduced comprehensive changes to legislation in England and Wales affecting the welfare of children. The Act:

• reinforces the autonomy of families through definition of parental responsibility; • provides for support from local authorities, in particular for families whose children are in need; and • legislates to protect children who may be suffering or are likely to suffer significant harm.

Annual reports on the progress of the Act were published by the Children Act Advisory Committee until 1997, but the Committee was then abolished. The Government is required to publish a report on the Act every 5 years, and statistics on its application are also available. There are also research reports on the operation of the Act (see Aldgate & Statham, 2001).

The main aims of the Act are:
• to bring together private and public law in one framework; • to achieve a better balance between protecting children and enabling parents to challenge state intervention; • to encourage greater partnership between statutory authorities and parents • to promote the use of voluntary arrangements;

• to restructure the framework of the courts to facilitate management of family proceedings.

The main principles and provisions embodied in this legislation are that: • the welfare of children must be the paramount consideration when the courts are making decisions about them; • the concept of parental responsibility has replaced that of parental rights; • children have the ability to be parties, separate from their parents, in legal proceedings; • local authorities are charged with duties to identify children in need and to safeguard and promote their welfare; • certain duties and powers are conferred upon local authorities to provide services for children and families; • a checklist of factors must be considered by the courts before reaching decisions; • orders under this Act should not be made unless it can be shown that this is better for the child than not making an order; • delay in deciding questions concerning children is likely to prejudice their welfare.

What changed with the Children Act 2004?
Following the death of eight-year old Victoria Climbié in 2000, the Government asked Lord Laming to conduct an inquiry (Laming, 2003) to help decide whether to introduce new legislation and guidance to improve the child protection system in England. The Government's response was the Keeping children safe report (DfES, DH and Home Office, 2003) and the Every Child Matters green paper (DfES, 2003), which led to the Children Act 2004. The Children Act 2004 does not replace or even amend much of the Children Act 1989. It covers England and Wales in separate sections. The Act:

creates the post of Children's Commissioner for England
places a duty on local authorities to appoint a director of children's services and an elected lead member for children's services, who is ultimately accountable for the delivery of services. The government published revised statutory guidance relating to the two posts in April 2012 (DfE, 2012)
places a duty on local authorities and their partners (including the police, health service providers and the youth justice system) to co-operate in promoting the wellbeing of children and young

people and to make arrangements to safeguard and promote the welfare of children states the creation of the new Local Safeguarding Children Boards (replacing the non-statutory Area Child Protection Committees) and gives them functions of investigation and review (sections 13 and 14), which they use to review all child deaths in their area updates the legislation on physical punishment (section 58) by limiting the use of the defence of reasonable punishment so that it can no longer be used when people are charged with the offences against a child of wounding, actual or grievous bodily harm or cruelty. Therefore any injury sustained by a child which is serious enough to warrant a charge of assault occasioning actual bodily harm cannot be considered to be as the result of reasonable punishment.

Amendment to the previous act also introduced the role of the LADO. The Local Authority Designated Officer (LADO) works within Children's Services to help safeguard children in accordance with the statutory guidance set out in Chapter 2: Organisational responsibilities of Working Together to Safeguard Children 2013. They should be informed of all cases in which it is alleged that a person who works with children has: • behaved in a way that has harmed, or may have harmed, a child; • possibly committed a criminal offence against children, or related to a child; or • behaved towards a child or children in a way that indicates they are unsuitable to work with children, for example if their conduct falls within any of these categories of abuse: • physical • sexual • emotional or • neglect. Once an allegation has been made, the LADO's role is to capture and co-ordinate the sharing of all the information relating to the case with the officers and agencies that need to be informed. The LADO will be involved from the initial phase, providing advice and guidance to the employer or voluntary organisation, and monitoring the progress of the case through to its conclusion.

CHILDCARE ACT 2006 - SUMMARY

The Childcare Act has four parts: duties on local authorities in England (Part 1); duties on local authorities in Wales (Part 2); regulation and inspection arrangements for childcare providers in England (Part 3); and general provisions (Part 4). Key provisions are as follows.

Sections 1-5 require local authorities and their NHS and Jobcentre Plus partners to work together to improve the outcomes of all children up to 5 and reduce inequalities between them, by ensuring early childhood services are integrated to maximise access and benefits to families - underpinning a Sure Start Children's Centre for every community

Sections 6, 8-11 & 13 require local authorities to assess the local childcare market and to secure sufficient childcare for working parents. Childcare will only be deemed sufficient if meets the needs of the community in general and in particular those families on lower incomes and those with disabled children. Local authorities take the strategic lead in their local childcare market, planning, supporting and commissioning childcare. Local authorities will not be expected to provide childcare direct but will be expected to work with local private, voluntary and independent sector providers to meet local need.

Section 7 re-enacts the duty for local authorities to secure a free minimum amount of early learning and care for all 3 and 4 year olds whose parents want it.

Section 12 extends the existing duty to provide information to parents, to ensure parents and prospective parents can access the full range of information they may need for their children right through to their 20th birthday. Local authorities will be required to ensure that this service is available to all parents and that it is pro-active in reaching those parents who might otherwise have difficulty accessing the information service.

Sections 39-48 introduce the Early Years Foundation Stage (EYFS) which will build on and bring together the existing Birth to Three Matters, Foundation Stage and national standards for under 8s day care and childminding. The EYFS will support providers in delivering high quality integrated early education and care for children from birth to age 5.

Sections 31-98 reform and simplify the framework for the regulation of childcare and early education to reduce bureaucracy and focus on raising quality and standards. All providers caring for children from birth to the 31 August following their fifth birthday will be required to register on the Early Years register and deliver the Early Years Foundation Stage (unless exceptionally exempted). Childcare settings providing for children from the 1 September following their firth birthday up to the age of eight must register on the compulsory part of the Ofsted Childcare Register (unless they are exempt.) The Act introduced certain requirements that all providers who are registering on the Ofsted Childcare Register will need to meet some of which are provided for in the Act but most of which are laid down in associated Regulations made under the Act.. Those childcare providers who are not obliged to register on the compulsory part of the Ofsted Childcare Register can choose to join the voluntary part of the Register. These providers will also need to meet certain requirements, which are laid down in Regulations made under the Act.

Sections 99-101 allow for the collection of information about young children to inform funding and support the local authority duties under the Act.

Every Child Matters
This is a Government Green Paper, the 'Every Child Matters' was published at the same time as the government's response to the report into the death of Victoria Climbie. Every Child Matters built on plans already in place to prevent the abuse of children, it focused on: Increasing the focus on supporting families and carers

Ensuring necessary intervention takes place before children reach crisis point Addressing the underlying problems identified in the report into the death of Victoria Climbie weak accountability and poor integration Ensuring that the people working with children are valued, rewarded and trained

After consultation, the government published Every Child Matter: Next Steps and passed the Children Act 2004, providing the legislation which could support the development of more effective, accessible services which focused on the needs of children, young people and their families. Every Child Matters: Change for Children (2004) outlines the government's approach to the well-being of children and young people from birth to age 19, or 24 for those with disabilities. The aim is that every child, whatever their background or circumstances should have the support they need to:

Be healthy
stay safe
enjoying and achieving
make a positive contribution
achieve economic well-being

Any organisations involved with providing services to children must genuinely work in partnership and share information, to protect children and young people from harm and help them achieve what they want in life. Emphasis is placed on the idea that, for each child to fulfil their potential, there must be a greater deal of co-operation, not only between Government agencies, but also between schools, GPs, Sports organisations and the Voluntary and Community sector. The Every Child Matters initiative provides a detailed framework for working with children within multi- agency partnerships. The themes covering health, safety, achievement of well- being and positive contribution making. One of the criticisms of services had been the failure of professionals to understand each other's roles or to work together in a multi- disciplinary manner and the ECM initiative sought to change this.

2. Understand how to respond to evidence or concerns that a child or young person has been abused or harmed.

Abuse and neglect are forms of maltreatment of a child. Somebody may abuse or neglect a child by inflicting harm, or by failing to act to prevent it. Children may be abused in a family or in an institutional or community setting, by somebody they know or more rarely by a stranger, for example, via the internet. They may be abused by adults or other children.

There are several different forms of abuse and here I will go through them.

Physical Abuse.

This may involve hitting, shaking, poisoning, burning, scalding, suffocating or any cause of physical harm to a child. Physical harm may also be caused by a parent or care giver fabricating the symptoms of, or deliberately inducing illness in a child.

Physical signs of physical abuse are:
Unexplained bruising
Multiple bruising to upper arms and outer thighs
Human bite marks
Fractures
Scalds

Some symptoms/signs and behaviours of physical abuse are:
Temper Outbursts
Fear of parent being approached
Depression
Withdrawn
Improbable excuses to explain injuries
Wearing inappropriate clothes for weather conditions to hide injuries Running away all the time
Fear of medical help or examination
Aggression towards others
Fear of physical contact shrinking back if touched
Self-destructive tendencies
Fear of suspected abuser being contacted

Sexual Abuse
Sexual abuse involves forcing or enticing a child or young person to take part in sexual activities. The activities may involve physical contact, including rape and oral sex or non-penetrative acts such as masturbation, kissing, rubbing and touching outside of clothing. They may also include non-contact activities such as involving children in looking at, or the production of images, watching sexual activities or encouraging children to act in sexually inappropriate ways and grooming them in preparation for abuse. Sexual abuse is not only perpetrated by males, women can also commit acts of sexual abuse, as can other children.

Physical signs of Sexual Abuse:
Bruising or bleeding near genital area
Pain or itching around genital area
Discomfort when walking or sitting
Pregnancy
Sexual transmitted disease
Stomach pains
Vaginal discharge or infection

Some of the symptoms/indicators and behaviours of sexual abuse are: Nightmares
Bed wetting
Easting problems
Aggressive or withdrawn
Drug/substance abuse
Unexplained sources of money or items
Being overly affectionate or knowledgeable in a sexual way inappropriate to the child's age Medical problems such as chronic itching, pain in the genitals, venereal diseases Depression, self-harm, suicide attempts, running away, overdoses, anorexia Personality changes such as becoming insecure or clingy

Regressing to younger behaviour patterns for example thumb sucking Becoming isolated or withdrawn
Inability to concentrate
Lack of trust or fear of someone they know well, for example not wanting to be alone with the babysitter Fear of clothing being removed
Suddenly drawing sexually explicit pictures

Emotional Abuse
Emotional abuse is the persistent maltreatment of a child that causes severe and adverse effects on the child's emotional development. It may involve conveying to children that they are worthless, unloved or inadequate. It may include not giving the child opportunity to express themselves, making fun of what they say or how they communicate or deliberately silencing them. It may involve serious bullying, including cyber bullying, causing children frequently to feel frightened or in danger, or the exploitation or corruption of children. Some level of emotional abuse is involved in all types of maltreatment of children, though it may occur alone. Signs of emotional abuse may include:

Failure to thrive
Development issues
Parents display little or no affection

Receive little attention from parents

Symptoms/indicators and behaviours of emotional abuse may include: Self-harm such as cutting
Fear of parent being approached
Speech disorders which develop suddenly
Developmental delay re emotional progress
Physical, mental and emotional development lags
Continual self-depreciation ('I'm stupid, I'm ugly etc') Overreaction to mistakes
Extreme fear of any new situation
Neurotic behaviour (rocking, hair twisting, self-mutilation) Extremes of passivity or aggression

Neglect

Neglect is the persistent failure to meet the child's basic physical and/or psychological needs, likely to result in the impairment of the child's health or development. Neglect may result in pregnancy as a result of maternal substance abuse. Once a child is born, neglect may involve a parent or care giver failing to: Provide adequate food, clothing or shelter

Protect a child from emotional or physical harm or danger
Ensure adequate supervision, including the use of inadequate care provision Ensure access to adequate to appropriate medical care or treatment It may also include neglect of a Childs basic emotional needs.

Physical signs of neglect may include:
Child dirty or smelly
Child constantly hungry
Child underweight
Inappropriately dressed for the weather

Symptoms/indicators and behaviours of neglect may be:
Constantly tired
Having few friends
Being left alone/unsupervised
Constant hunger
Poor personal hygiene
Poor state of clothing
Emaciation
Untreated medical problems
No social relationships
Compulsive scavenging
Destructive tendencies

Bullying

Under the Children Act 1989 an incident of bullying should be treated as child protection when a child is suffering or likely to suffer significant harm under the Equalities Act 2010 public bodies, which includes schools must address and eliminate unlawful discrimination, harassment and victimisation. Bullying is not always easy to recognise and can take a number of forms. They can be bullying attacks that are physical (pushing, hitting, pinching and other forms of or violence) or the can be verbal (name calling, sarcasm, spreading rumours, persistent teasing, ridiculing, humiliating).

Signs of bullying can include:
Depression
Low self esteem
Shyness
Isolation
Poor academic achievement
Threatened or attempted suicide

Symptoms/indicators and behaviours of a bullied child may include: Coming home with cuts and bruises
Torn clothes
Losing dinner money
Being moody or bad tempered
Asking for stolen possessions to be replaced
Falling out with previously good friends
Wanting to avoid leaving home
Aggression with siblings
Sleep problems
Anxiety
Being less well at school
Becoming quiet and withdrawn

2.2 Describe the actions to take if a child or young person alleges harm or abuse in line with policies and procedures of own setting.

Recognising child abuse is not easy and it is not our responsibility to decide if abuse has taken place or not, but we do have a responsibility and duty of care to act in order that the appropriate agencies can investigate and take any necessary action to protect a child.

The DFES guidance entitled 'What to do if you're worried a child is being abused – summary' advises that you should: Be familiar with and follow your organisation's procedures and protocols for promoting and safeguarding the welfare of children in your area, and know who to contact in your organisation to express concerns about a child's welfare. Remember that an allegation of child abuse or neglect or neglect may lead to a criminal investigation, so don't do anything that may jeopardise a police investigation. Ensure that you know who is responsible for making referrals and if it is your responsibility know who to contact in police, health, education, school and children's social care to express concerns about a child's welfare. When referring a child to children's social services you should consider and include any information on the child's development needs and their parents/carers capacity to respond to these needs within the context of their wider family environment. See the child and ascertain their wishes and feelings as part of considering what action to take in relation to the child's welfare. Communicate with the child in a way that is appropriate to their age and understanding, especially if the child is disabled and for children whose first language is not English. Depending on the substance and seriousness of the concerns you may require advice from the police or children's social care to ensure you do not jeopardise the safety of the child or any subsequent investigation. It is important to reassure the child however you must not promise confidentiality. Record full information about the child including their name, address, gender, date of birth, name/s of person/s with parental responsibility (for consent purposes) and primary carer if different. Keep this information up to date. Record all concerns, discussions about the child, the decisions that were made and reasons for those decisions in writing. The child's records should include an up to date account, and details of the lead worker in the relevant agencies, for example social worker, teacher or health visitor. Knowing how damaging abuse is to children it is up to the adults around them to take responsibility for stopping it. If you are concerned or a child tells you about abuse you must report it immediately. The following can be contacted through your telephone directory: Police

Social Services
Samaritans 0345 909090
NSPCC 0800 800 500
ISPCC 00 353 742 9744
ChildLine 0800 1111
Parentline 0808 800 2222
In 1991 the United Nations Convention on the Rights if the Child 1989 was sanctioned in the UK and included the following rights for children: The right to protection from abuse
The right to express their views
The right to be listened to
The right to care and services for disabled children or children living away from home The right to protection from any form of discrimination
The right to receive and share information as long as that information is not damaging to others The right to freedom of religion
The right to education

The law has now given children a voice and as stated in the Children's Act 2004, the best interest of the child is paramount in all considerations of welfare (convention of the rights of the child 1989 - Article 3). Children should be protected from all forms of violence (Convention of the rights of the child 1989 – Article 19) Children should be separated from their parents if they have been abused or neglected (Convention of the rights of the child 1989 – Article 19). This can cause tensions with child's parents as this is irrespective of what they think. The child does have a right to confidentiality during investigations but the care worker should also make it clear that they have a duty of care to protect and safeguard the child which may mean sharing information with others, on a strictly need to know basis.

Case study CU3119 Understanding Safeguarding of Children and Young People for Those Working in the Adult Sector

Candidate Name: xxxxxxxxxxxx
As we are a provider that carries out a regulated service we have to be registered with Care Quality Commission. We have to take into account the Care Quality Commission Essential standards quality and safety, which is a guide to help providers of health and social care to comply with the Health and Social Care Act 2008 (Regulated Activities) Regulation 2010 and the Care Quality Commission (Registration) Regulation 2009. These regulations describe the essential standards of quality and safety that people who use health and adult care services have a right to expect. The Care Quality Commission will continuously monitor our service to ensure that we are meeting the essential standards and if they have any concerns that at any time we was not meeting the essential standards of quality and safety they will act quickly, working closely with commissioners and others,

and using their enforcement powers to bring about improvements if our service was poor or to prevent us from carrying out regulated activities.

The Health and Social Care Act 2008 (Regulated Activities) Regulations 2010 Regulation 11 and The Care Quality Commission Essential standards quality and safety Outcome 7 safeguarding people who use services from abuse what these regulations say?

ϖAs a registered person I must make suitable arrangements to ensure that service users are safeguarded against the risk of abuse by means of:

- Taking reasonable steps to identify the possibility of abuse and prevent it before it occurs
- Responding appropriately to any allegation of abuse.

ϖWhere any form of control or restraint is used in carrying on of the regulated activity, the registered person must have suitable arrangements in place to protect service users against the risk of such control of restraint being:

- Unlawful
- Otherwise excessive

ϖFor the purpose of paragraph 1 "abuse" in relation to a service user, means:

- Sexual abuse
- Physical or physical or psychological ill treatment
- Theft, misuse or misappropriation of money or property
- Neglect and acts of omission which cause harm or place at risk of harm

A person who uses care services can be protected from abuse or the risk of abuse when service providers comply with these regulations they will:

- Take action to identify and prevent abuse from happening in their service •Respond appropriately when it is suspected that abuse has occurred or there is a risk of occurring •Ensure that Government and local guidance about safeguarding people from abuse is accessible to all staff and out into practice •Make sure that the use of restraint is always appropriate, reasonable, proportionate and justifiable to the individual •Only use de-escalation or restraint in a way that respects dignity and protects human rights. Where possible respect the preferences of people who uses the services •Understand how diversity, beliefs and values of people who uses services may be influence the identification, prevention and response to safeguarding concerns •Protect others from negative effect of any behaviour by people who use the service •Where applicable, only use Deprivation of Liberty Safeguarding when it is in the best interests of people who uses the service and in accordance with the Mental Capacity Act 2005

The rights of vulnerable adults to live a life free from neglect, exploitation and abuse are protected by The Human Rights Act 1998. Specifically, a vulnerable adult's right to life is protected (under Article 2) their right to be protected from inhuman and degrading treatment (under Article 3) and their right to liberty and security (under Article 5).

Vulnerable adults are protected in the same way as any other person against criminal acts. Where there is reasonable suspicion that a criminal offence may have occurred it is the responsibility of the police to investigate and make a decision about any subsequent action.

In the past safeguarding practices was mostly commonly applied to children and young people under the age of eighteen, but due to key aspects of legislation being extended to include similar standards of protection to vulnerable adults. There are a number of legislations regulations and professional guidance for safe working with children and young people below are some of them:

- The Children Act (1989)
- the Rehabilitation of Offenders Act 1974
- The Protection of Children Act (1999)
- The Data Protection Act (1998)
- The Children Act (Every Child Matters) (2004)
- The Mental Capacity Act Code of Practice (DH 2007)
- The Mental Health ct Code of Practice (DH 2008)
- The Health and Social Care Act 2008 (Regulated Activities) Regulations 2019 •The Deprivation of Liberty safeguarding (DH 2009)
- Violence : The short term management of violence/disturbed behaviour in in-patient psychiatric and emergency departments (CG25 NICE 2005) •The Human Rights Act (1998)
- The Sexual Offences Act (2003)
- The Protection of Freedoms Act 2012
- The Criminal Justice Court Services Act (2000)
- The Equalities Act (2010)
- Working Together To Safeguard Children (revised HMG 2006) •What to do if you are Worried a Child is Being Abused (HMG 2006) •Guidance on when to suspect child maltreatment (CC89 NICE 2009) •The Framework for the Assessment of Children in Need and their Families (DOH 2000) •The Common Assessment Framework for Children and Young People: A Guide for Practitioners (CWDC 2010) •Safeguarding Adults (2005)

- Services for people with learning disabilities and challenging behaviour or mental health needs- Mansell report: revised edition (DH 2007) •What to do if you're worried a child is being abused (HMG 2006) •Healthy Lives brighter futures: The Children's strategy (DH 2009) •Guidance for restrictive physical intervention (HMG 2002) •Statutory guidance on making arrangements to safeguard and promote the welfare of children under section 11 of the Children Act 2004 (HMG 2007) •Information Sharing: Guidance for Practitioners and Managers (DCSF 2008) •Independent Safeguarding Authority

- No Secrets (DH and Home Office 2000)
- The Safeguarding Vulnerable Groups Act 2006

Our organisation has a written safeguarding vulnerable adult policy that is supported by robust procedures and guidelines. Our policy acknowledges that all adults have the right to live a life free from neglect abuse and exploitation, it outlines the organisational commitment to uphold these right by creating and maintaining an environment which aims to ensure as far as possible that adults who live at the home are kept free from abuse and exploitation, and is explicit about the organisation's zero-tolerance of abuse wherever it occurs. Our safeguarding vulnerable adult policy is supported by robust procedures and guidelines.

By having a culture of inclusion, transparency and openness means that we have nothing to hide and that it is open to feedback from vulnerable adults, staff, volunteers with a view it improve how we carry out our activities and deliver our services. As the manager I have to ensure that the organisation operates effectively, I can gain valuable insights or to learn lesions through the support and supervision processes, and from the feedback from satisfaction survey.

Our safeguarding policy statement is clearly displayed to ensure that every one who is involved with the organisation including management staff volunteers vulnerable adults advocates and visitors are aware that the policy exists, what it aims to achieve and the steps that will be taken to achieve those aims. The primary aim of our safeguarding policy is to manage the risk of abuse to vulnerable adults by establishing a culture in which the rights of vulnerable adults are fully respected and by putting in place a range of procedures which supports that culture. By establishing a culture, which is mindful of and has a zero tolerance of abuse wherever it occurs and whoever causes it, and by having in place robust procedures are all part of our organisation risk reducing armoury. By properly implementing our safeguarding policy it has the potential to reduce both the likelihood and impact of abuse by:

•Having a good recruitment and selection practice that prevents unsuitable people from joining the company •All staff/volunteers have to have a DBS and a ISA before they can start work •Ensuring that staff and volunteers are aware of the indicators of vulnerability and risk and the possible signs of abuse •Ensuring that staff and volunteers are equipped to respond to concerns about actual, alleged or suspected abuse •Ensure that staff and volunteers are properly trained, supported and supervised in their work with vulnerable adults •Ensure that staff and volunteers know what constitutes acceptable behaviour and good practice and that they are supported when they challenge poor practices •Promoting a culture of inclusion, transparency and openness throughout the organisation and its services and activities •Making sure that staff and volunteers are aware of how information about vulnerable adults should be handled •Having in place a good overall management and practice support by the range of policies and procedures

In addition to a safeguarding vulnerable adult policy we have a range of organisational policies and procedures aimed at promoting safe and healthy working practices. These are necessary to ensure that my organisation is properly managed, that the resources both human and financial are being used efficiently and effectively and that my service will maintain the public confidence.

Some of the relevant policies are:

•Health and Safety
•Moving and Handling
•First Aid
•Fire Safety
•Equal Opportunities
•Handling vulnerable adults money
•Bullying/Harassment
•Violence in the workplace
•Whistle blowing
•Recruitment and selection of staff/volunteers
•Recognising, responding to, recording and reporting concerns about abuse •Recording and reporting and reviewing accidents, incidents and near misses •Risk assessments and management

- Volunteers
- Advocates
- Management of records, confidentially and sharing of information •Receiving comments and suggestions and management of concerns and complaints •Staff supervision

As we provide a service that is regulated we are required to be registered with the Care Quality Commission. Section 23(1) of the Health and Social Care Act 2008 required the Care Quality Commission to produce guidance about compliance (the Essential standards of quality and safety) to help providers of health and social care to help them comply with the regulations within the Act that govern their activities. The Act, the regulation and the guidance are part of a wider regulatory framework to ensure that people who use services are protected and receive the care, treatment and support that they need.

To ensure that everyone is clear what my organisation is trying to achieve and what their particular roles are we have a thorough induction process to ensure that all new staff/volunteers are properly prepared for their work and to reduce their anxieties associated with starting a new post/role. Induction takes place when a new member of staff or volunteer starts work with us it includes:

- Information regarding the organisational policies, procedures, guidelines, activities an ethos •What is expected and required of them and the boundaries or limits within which they should operate •An awareness raising and training on the recognition, recording and reporting abuse

Induction is done over a few days as new staff/volunteers can only take in a certain amount of information at a time and to ensure that everything is covered during an induction I use a checklist.

All new staff/volunteers have their own training programme that takes into account their skills, knowledge and experience and then training would be provided where gaps was identify.

Our safeguarding training includes:

- A basic awareness and understanding of the factors which contribute to vulnerability •The possible signs of vulnerable adult abuse
- How to respond when abuse is disclosed or suspected
- Recording and reporting procedures
- Information about confidentiality in the context of adult safeguarding •Staff are trained to take concerns about adult abuse seriously •How to deal with information about alleged or suspected abuse sensitively •Staff know never to make promises to keep secrets

- Staff know that their role is not to investigate
- Staff know how to report their concerns about alleged or suspected abuse

Our safeguarding policy is also supported by a code of behaviour that has been tailored to my service it is essential to establish a set of ground rules, it contains a statement about how staff/volunteers are expected to behave towards vulnerable adults. It is specific to certain activities examples:

- Handling vulnerable adults money
- Photography

- Physical intervention and restraint
- Physical contact and intimate care
- Unacceptable behaviour

Our Code of Behaviour is used as a training tool during induction where each element is explained and discussed with new staff and volunteers. I have also used it as a framework for discussion in support and supervision sessions and ongoing training.

Our safeguarding policy procedures, guidelines and Code of Behaviour are regular review to ensure that they are fit for purpose.

As we work with vulnerable adults it is important to reassure them that we are committed to good practice in keeping them safe from harm and exploitation and upholding their rights that is we would always act in their best interest and with their consent our safeguarding policy sets out how we will do this. Our practice and our safeguarding policy is underpinned and guided by a number of values and principles which are:

- Access to information and knowledge
- Choice
- Confidentiality
- Consent
- Dignity and respect
- Equality and diversity
- Fulfilment
- Independence
- Privacy
- Safety
- Support

It is not easy to identify abuse sometimes the nature of abuse is not visible and/or often the person being abused is afraid to speak out, however there are some more common signs of abuse which if seen, may suggest that abuse has occurred example: •Multiple bruising that cannot be easily explained

- Deterioration of health for no apparent reason
- Sudden and unusual weight loss
- Inappropriate or inadequate clothing
- Withdrawal or mood changes
- A carer who is unwilling to allow access to the person
- A person who is unwilling or unhappy about being left alone with a particular carer •Unexplained shortage or disappearance of money

Any of the above signs may indicate that abuse is happening Types of abuse:
- Physical including hitting, slapping, kicking, the misuse of medication, restraint or inappropriate sanctions •Psychological including threats of harm or abandonment, forced marriage, deprivation of contact, humiliation, blaming, controlling, intimidation. Coercion, harassment, verbal abuse, isolation or withdrawal from services or supportive networks •Emotional abuse where there is a persistent lack of love or affection, frequent taunting or being shouted at, experiencing any of the other categories of abuse •Sexual abuse such as rape, sexual assault or sexual acts to which

vulnerable adults has not or could not have consented, or to which they were pressurised into consenting • Financial abuse such as theft, fraud or exploitation, pressure in connection with wills, property or inheritance, misuse of property, possessions or benefits •Neglect such as ignoring medical or physical care needs and preventing access to health, social care or education services or withholding the necessities of life such as food, drink and heating discriminatory abuse such as that based on race or sexuality or a person's disability and other forms of harassment or slurs •Institutional abuse can sometimes happen in residential homes, nursing homes or hospitals when people are mistreated because of poor or inadequate care, neglect and poor practice that affect the whole of that service Bulling is another form of abuse and can take many forms. It is repeated harassment over a period of time, and is done in a way that makes it difficult for the person being bullied to defend themselves •Bullying behaviour can occur anywhere especially if supervision is inadequate •It is an abuse which can take many forms from simple verbal taunts and persistent teasing to humiliation and physical abuse There are three main types of bullying

- Verbal bullying
- Physical bullying
- Indirect bullying

All signs of bullying must be taken seriously.
Risk to a vulnerable adult is known to be greater when:

- The vulnerable adult is emotionally or socially isolated •A pattern of violence exists or has existed in the past
- Drugs or alcohol are being misused
- Relationships are placed under stress

When care services are provided abuse is more likely to occur if staff/volunteers are:

- Inadequately trained
- Poorly supervised
- Lacking support or work in isolation

In addition to these risk factors there are a range of other factors that increase the likelihood of abuse:

- Where an illness causes unpredictable behaviour
- Where the person is experiencing communication difficulties •Where the person concerned demands more than the carer can offer •Where the family circumstances changes e.g. death of a partner •Where a carer has been forced to change their lifestyle as a result of becoming a carer •Where a carer becomes isolated and is offered no relief from a demanding role •Where other relationships are unstable or placed under pressure whilst caring •Where there is persistent financial problems exist

- Where a partner abuses drugs and/or alcohol
- Where a victim seeks to disclose abuse gets support or leave an abusive relationship

If a vulnerable adult was to disclose abuse to a staff member or volunteers they would:

- Stay calm and not show shock or disbelief

- They would listen carefully to what they are saying
- They would be sympathetic
- They would be aware of the possibility that medical evidence might be required •They would tell the person that they have done the right thing in telling them •Tell the person that they are treating this information seriously •Inform the person that it was not their fault

- Inform the person that they are going to inform the appropriate person •Staff would take steps to protect and support the person •They would report the allegation of abuse to their manager or to social services or to the police

Staff would:

- Not press the person for more details
- Not stop the person who is freely recalling significant events as they may not tell them again •Not ask leading questions that could be interpreted as putting words or suggestions to vulnerable adults or any vulnerable witnesses •Not to make promises to keep secrets as this kind of information confidential •Not to make promises they cannot keep

- Not to contact the alleged abuser
- Not to be judgmental
- Not pass on information to anyone other than those with a legitimate need to know

At the first opportunity make a note of the disclosure with the aim to:

- Note what was said, using exact words and phrases spoken, wherever possible •Describe the circumstances in which the disclosure came about •Note the setting and anyone else who was there at the time •Separate out factual information from their own opinion

- Use a pen or biro with black ink so that their report can be photocopied •Their report may be required later as part of a legal action or disciplinary procedure

Abuse can occur in situations where another adult, sometimes a family member or friend or care worker, misuses a position of trust and power over a vulnerable adult. It is important that vulnerable adults are made aware of their rights and sources of support and information which they can draw upon if they feel uncomfortable or threatened. By sharing information with vulnerable adults and by actively working towards raising their confidence, involving them in decision making, taking their views and concerns seriously and if a vulnerable adult has been abused ensuring that they receive support and protection from further abuse.

Our organisation has a whistle blowing policy that makes it clear that:

- We take poor or malpractice seriously it gives examples of the types of concerns to be raised. To ensure that the whistle blowing concern is clearly distinguished from a grievance •Staff or volunteers have the option to raise concerns outside of their line management structure •Staff or volunteers are able to access confidential advice from an independent source •Where possible the organisation will respect the confidentiality of a member of staff raising a concern •When and how the concerns may be raised outside the organisation •If it is a disciplinary matter both to victimise a bona fide whistleblower and for someone to maliciously make a false allegation

It is important that staff/volunteers are aware of and have confidence in the organisation whistle blowing procedure.

We have a procedure for reporting and recording accidents, incidents and near misses that occur. These may involve vulnerable adults, staff members or volunteers, staff and volunteers need to know our procedure for reporting and recording. Accidents, incidents and near misses particularly those which are recurring, can be indicators of organisation risk, including a risk to safeguarding which needs to be managed. Where the accident, incident or near miss is in some way connected to a safeguarding matter, or if they have any concerns about an individual safety and welfare or the safety of others, that they need to pass on this information to myself as their manager so that I can take the appropriate action.

Our safeguarding policy states how information relating to a vulnerable adult or concerns about a vulnerable adult should be confidential and shared on a need to know basis only. All staff or volunteers are clear that information relating to a concern, disclosure or allegation or suspicion should not be discussed inside or outside the organisation, other than those e.g. manager who need to know. It is essential that we have a robust system in place for the maintenance of all records, including records of abuse or suspected abuse. If I was alerted about a concern about a vulnerable adult I would ensure that the vulnerable adult is in no immediate danger and that any medical or police assistance required has been sought if it was clear from the information available that there is a specific allegation of abuse I would need to act promptly and in accordance with the agreed reporting procedure which would state what action I need to take.

If I need to make a referral the information that I required would be:

- The name
- The date of birth
- Gender
- The address
- Ethnic Origin
- Client group
- Other agencies that the vulnerable adult is known to
- Details about the allegation
- The person raising the concern
- Location of abuse
- The need for medical treatment if any
- The reason for suspicions of abuse or type of abuse
- A brief description of the allegation/abuse including dates and times
- Any action that I have taken
- Any other information that I might consider useful to an investigation that relates to the alleged perpetrator and his/her location and whether or not the vulnerable adult is aware of/has agreed to the referral

Details about the alleged perpetrator

- Their name and address
- Their age if known
- Their gender

- Their relationship with the vulnerable adult

I would need to complete an alert form which is called an AP1 form if the vulnerable adult is known to social services I would send it to their care manager if not known I would send the form to the contact centre so they can open up a referral which would then makes that person known to social services who will assess the alert and determine what action is required e.g. to raise an investigation and make a refer to other agencies e.g. police if they consider it to be a criminal offensive, vulnerable adults are protected in the same way as any other person against criminal acts and is dealt with through the criminal justice system.

I have to consider if the concern is a safeguarding issue or not this would involve checking out the information or concern. If I consider it is not a safeguarding issue and no referral has been made to the statutory authority I would document the concern recording details of my action taken and my reason for not making the referral however I would need to monitor the situation on an ongoing basic.

Printed in Great Britain
by Amazon